SpringerBriefs in Finance

For further volumes:
http://www.springer.com/series/10282

Roberto Ruozi · Pierpaolo Ferrari

Liquidity Risk Management in Banks

Economic and Regulatory Issues

 Springer

Roberto Ruozi
Department of Finance
Bocconi University
Milan
Italy

Pierpaolo Ferrari
Department of Business
University of Brescia
Brescia
Italy

10 07101435

ISSN 2193-1720   ISSN 2193-1739   (electronic)
ISBN 978-3-642-29580-5 ISBN 978-3-642-29581-2   (eBook)
DOI 10.1007/978-3-642-29581-2
Springer Heidelberg New York Dordrecht London

Library of Congress Control Number: 2012945483

Printed on acid-free paper

Springer is part of Springer Science+Business Media (www.springer.com)

Contents

**Liquidity Risk Management in Banks: Economic
and Regulatory Issues** 1
  1   Introduction 2
  2   Banks and Liquidity Risk............................ 3
  3   Liquidity Risk: Economic Issues 7
       3.1   The Impact Area of the Liquidity Risk 9
       3.2   The Timeframe of the Risk Analysis................ 11
       3.3   The Origin of the Risk 12
       3.4   The Economic Scenario of the Risk 13
       3.5   Models and Measurement Techniques 14
       3.6   Organisational Processes and Structures............. 22
  4   Liquidity Risk: Regulatory Issues 26
       4.1   Common Principles for Sound Liquidity Management
            and Supervision 28
       4.2   Minimum Liquidity Standards 29
       4.3   Monitoring Tools to Assess Liquidity Risk 41
  5   Economic and Managerial Effects of the New Regulation 41
       5.1   The Impact on Profitability 42
       5.2   The Effects on Bank Assets Composition
            and the Business Mix 43
       5.3   The Effects on Bank Liabilities 46
       5.4   The Substitution Effects Between Banking
            and Financial Products......................... 47
       5.5   The Further Loss of Market Share in Favour of
            the So-Called "Shadow Banks" 48
  6   Conclusions 50
  References 51

Liquidity Risk Management in Banks: Economic and Regulatory Issues

Abstract At the international level, a wide consensus has emerged over many years on the importance of liquidity monitoring and the need to mitigate the associated risk in order to preserve the stability of individual banks and the soundness of the entire banking system. However, many differences have also emerged regarding how this principle has been transposed into rules or guidelines. Although the changes that have occurred in the international banking system in these last decades have increased the technical solutions available to banks in managing liquidity risk, these changes have also led to an underestimation of the actual exposure to this risk. The crisis has highlighted the need for more efficient liquidity management by banks by involving all governing bodies and corporate management in monitoring and managing liquidity in both normal and stress conditions, integrating better treasury with other functions affecting the liquidity position, and increasing the importance of liquidity risk as a part of risk management. The crisis has also highlighted the weaknesses of self-regulation based on internal models and the need to integrate domestic and international regulations in order to take into account that the search for bank stability and the reduction of competitive inequalities also require defining common rules to limit banks' appetite for liquidity risk. Liquidity risk is difficult to measure and depends on so many factors that a capital requirement is unsuitable to prevent it. Proper management policy requires examining the liquidity risk as a function of the impact area, the time horizon, the origin and the economic scenario where it occurs. After analysing these four aspects, it is necessary to define models of risk measurement, by identifying indicators to monitor, setting appropriate operating limits and related organisational issues. After reviewing the main economic aspects of liquidity risk, this study examines the new international regulations which will introduce, albeit gradually, a common framework for liquidity risk management in banks, and highlights the main economic and managerial consequences that these regulations will produce for bank management.

R. Ruozi and P. Ferrari, *Liquidity Risk Management in Banks*,
SpringerBriefs in Finance, DOI: 10.1007/978-3-642-29581-2_1,
© The Author(s) 2013

Keywords Liquidity · Liquidity risk · Funding liquidity risk · Market liquidity risk · Regulation · Basel III

Jel Codes G01 · G21 · G28

1 Introduction

The financial crisis of 2007 that triggered the turmoil in the financial markets has demonstrated the central role that effective processes for managing liquidity risk play in maintaining both the stability of individual banks and the soundness of the entire banking system in the event of unexpected crises of a systemic nature.

Liquidity risk is difficult to measure and depends on so many factors that a defence based on capital requirement is ill-suited to prevent it.

A sound management policy requires examining liquidity risk as a function of the impact area, the timeframe, the origin, and the economic scenarios where it occurs. After analysing these four aspects, it is necessary to define models of risk measurement, by identifying indicators to monitor and setting appropriate operating limits that allow advance detection of any potential liquidity crisis.

Whether in the short- or medium-long term, each bank must choose between methods for modelling cash flows relative to on- and off-balance sheet items, with particular attention paid to those items characterised by a contingent nature in their use or the repayments by bank customers.

The different methodologies must hypothesise both normal operating circumstances, characterised by a stable market situation and stressed scenarios, with liquidity shortage at the bank level or at the systemic level.

The associated organisational aspects are also complex and vary according to the models adopted by the individual banks and, above all, by the banking groups they belong to.

Regardless of the methodology used and the organisational models adopted, the choices regarding liquidity risk management reflect the risk appetite of each bank. In a period of growing internationalization of banking systems, with the consequent increase in competitive pressures, each bank has been obliged to strike a delicate equilibrium between a prudent and balanced maturity structure of assets and liabilities and the pursuit of increasing profitability levels. As a consequence, this has given rise to very different liquidity risk exposures across countries and between different banks within each country.

Moreover, defining the most efficient regulatory framework and supervisory approach for liquidity risk management is not easy. For many years there has been a broad agreement, at the international level, on the importance of liquidity monitoring and the need to mitigate the associated risk in order to ensure the stability of the financial system. Nevertheless, there are many differences in the procedures by which this evaluation is transposed into regulations or guidelines. While some supervisory authorities have set quantitative limits to liquidity risk exposure, other authorities have placed greater trust on defences of a qualitative nature, based on internal measurement and reporting systems.

It is evident, however, that the differences in the regulatory and supervisory approaches are also derived from context-specific factors that characterise the different jurisdictions that do not have a secondary effect in terms of mitigating a potential liquidity crisis. These factors include rules governing deposit insurance schemes, central bank policies to supply liquidity and lending of last resort, bankruptcy law and, last but not least, the structural and functional characteristics of each banking system.

2 Banks and Liquidity Risk

The management of a bank is subject to an indispensable liquidity constraint, like any other type of company. Yet it is typical of banks that this constraint assumes a more stringent and severe nature, due to the peculiarities of the functions performed and the specific operations carried out by banks.

The operation of a bank is closely dependent on the systematic acceptance of its liabilities by creditors and on the expectation that its commitments will always find a detailed confirmation. In this respect, the liquidity for the bank takes on an essentially protective meaning that is able to continuously ensure a state of technical solvency. In fact, the insolvency of the bank may be caused by technical circumstances related to insufficient cash reserves and by economic circumstances related to the inadequacy of the equity value. Indeed, there is a close connection and a relationship of alternative priority between these causative factors.[1]

During ordinary management, a bank is solvent if the three following conditions occur simultaneously:

- The ability to cope immediately, in both normal and stress conditions, with any request for payment emerging from a contractual obligation either contingent or non-contingent for which customers can withdraw money. This depends above all, in the short term, on the availability of adequate cash reserves, as well as on the adoption of effective monitoring processes and appropriate operating systems that are able to meet any unexpected cash outflows;
- The ability to maintain a constant balance in the medium-long term between monetary inflows and outflows. This capacity depends mainly on the containment of the degree of maturity transformation operated by the bank and on the presence of a harmonious juxtaposition between the weighted average maturity of assets and weighted average maturity of liabilities, as well as on the proper management of cash flows arising from off-balance sheet items;

---

[1] The relation between liquidity and leverage can be found in: Adrian and Shin (2008).

- The ability to absorb any losses without jeopardizing the rights of creditors. The greater the amount of equity, the lower the probability that the market value of assets falls below the market value of debts, resulting in a state of insolvency for the bank. However, as is known, since identical volumes of activity can incorporate very different levels of risk, it becomes essential to correlate the amount of overall risk borne by the bank with the minimum capital that it must hold.[2]

On this third condition, for a long time there has been evidence of the need to adopt common tools across several countries that are intended to detect the stability of banks and the soundness of the entire banking system and reduce competitive inequalities among internationally active banks. This objective was achieved in 1988 through the introduction of a risk-related minimum capital ratio, which in later years has become increasingly sophisticated and better able, although not without limitations, to capture more precisely the actual size of the risks borne by banks and the resulting minimum capital base.

On the first two conditions, conversely, there has never been any attempt to achieve a uniform international regulation to reduce competitive inequalities among internationally active banks in different jurisdictions. These inequalities arise not only from the presence of different capital levels but also from more rigid and more profitable assets structures, less stable and cheaper liabilities structures and differing degrees of maturity transformation.

Although a broad consensus has emerged at the international level on the importance of the supervision of liquidity and the need to mitigate the risk associated with it in order to ensure the stability of the financial system, in practice there have been many differences in the ways in which these principles have been transposed into rules or guidelines. Some supervisors have set quantitative limits to the exposure to liquidity risk. Others have increased the reliance on principles of a qualitative nature, based on internal risk management systems.[3]

The risk of failing to meet the bank's cash commitments on time and in a cost-effective manner depends on so many factors—the maturity structure of assets, the maturity structure of liabilities, characteristics of loans and other assets, funding features and instruments, off-balance sheet dynamics, changes in costs and revenues that affect monetary outflows and inflows, the creditworthiness of the bank, money and capital market conditions—that a defence based on a capital requirement is unsuited to its attenuation, and more effective monitoring of all these factors and the adoption of consistently management decisions are needed.[4]

However, the practices adopted by banks in a context of self-regulation have shown many weaknesses. If, on the one hand, the recent changes in the international banking system have increased the technical solutions available to banks to

---

[2] Ruozi (2011).

[3] Vento and La Ganga (2009).

[4] On the relation between liquidity risk and the various subcategories of risk defined by Basel II, see: CEBS (2008), p. 12.

manage the liquidity risk, on the other hand, they have led to an underestimation of the actual exposure to this risk. The crisis has highlighted the need for more efficient liquidity management by banks through the involvement of all governing bodies and corporate management in monitoring and managing liquidity in both normal and stress conditions, a greater integration of treasury with other functions that affect the liquidity position, and the increased importance of liquidity risk as a part of risk management.[5]

While it is true—to paraphrase Tolstoy—that profitable banks are all alike and that every bank in crisis is in crisis in its own way, it is clear that—beyond the determinants of the crisis situation—the insolvency of a bank results from either economic circumstances related to the inadequacy of the available capital or technical circumstances related to poor management of liquidity risk in the short or medium-long term.

The different maturity structure of assets (mainly medium and long term) and liabilities (mostly short term) generates the risk that the bank is unable to respond promptly to requests for payment by its customers. Alternatively, to honour such claims, the bank may be forced to quickly sell a high volume of financial assets in its portfolio, accepting a price below the current market value. Such situations can be traced to the different notions of liquidity risk: the events of the summer of 2007, such as the sudden scarcity of funds in the interbank market and the queues of depositors outside branches of a British bank, made evident the strong under-estimation of liquidity risk not only by banks but also by the supervisory authorities in most countries.

Even today, many observers deem it inappropriate to define an internationally consistent regulatory framework based on prudential requirements to limit liquidity risk-taking by banks, and consider the presence of more stringent regu-lation of capital adequacy to be sufficient. The consequent improvement in the quality of capital composition, the more effective business risk measurement and the new criteria for calculation of risk-weighted assets would put an end to the regulatory arbitrage practices that have existed up to now.[6] The management of liquidity risk is considered by those observers to be a component of corporate strategy and the result of the risk appetite of the bank, whose stability depends only on the presence of an adequate volume of high quality capital in relation to risk-weighted assets.

However, this view overlooks the fact that the insolvency of a bank is the result of not only economic reasons but also technical reasons, due to improper man-agement of liquidity and the consequent risks taken in the short and medium-long term. At the same time, this view ignores the competitive disparities between banks with a balanced maturity structure of assets and liabilities and those with highly unbalanced funding structures. To support this statement, Fig. 1 shows the maturity structure of the assets and liabilities of Northern Rock in late September

---

[5] Senior Supervisors Group (2009).

[6] IIF (2010), EBF (2010), Blundell-Wignall and Atkinson (2010).

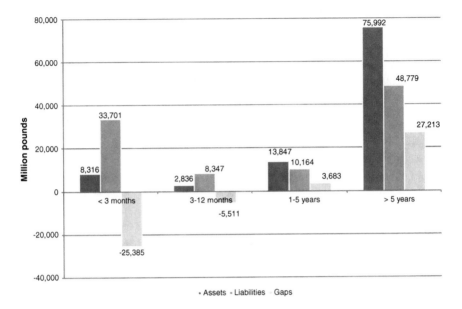

Fig. 1 Northern Rock maturity mismatches as of September 2007. *Source* Based on Onado (2009)

2007 and the resulting gap between assets and liabilities along the four identified time bands. It reveals how, over a period of 3 months, there was a gap between assets and liabilities with maturity within 3 months of over 25 billion pounds. Reasoning on the 0–12 months cumulative gap, the difference between assets and liabilities with a residual maturity within the year amounted to almost 31 billion compared to total assets that amounted, at the same date, to almost 101 billion pounds.

Besides the fact that this was certainly not the only cause of the Northern Rock crisis, those who believe it unwise to define a common regulation of liquidity risk across countries based on prudential requirements should consider that the maturity structure of assets and liabilities of that bank was perfectly compatible with and respectful of the law then in force, as the regulation assumed the proper functioning of the interbank market and took equally for granted the continuation of an infinite originate-to-distribute model in which the loan made by the bank is not held until maturity in its banking book, but is transferred to others through loan sale operations or, more frequently, through securitisation.[7]

Even though the common framework for liquidity risk, in addition to the new regulation on capital requirement, makes it possible to achieve the objectives of the stability of banks and the entire banking system and the reduction of competitive inequalities among banks, the fact remains that the establishment of a

---

[7] Bruni and Llewellyn (2009).

common framework is undoubtedly very complex and that the current version developed by the Basel Committee, as will be shown in more detail, suffers from many limitations and requires careful and effective calibration before its full entry into force.

3 Liquidity Risk: Economic Issues

Liquidity risk is the potential inability of a bank to meet punctually and in a cost-effective way its envisaged contractual payment obligations when they fall due.

The aims of liquidity risk management are:

- To ensure at all times an adequate corresponding balance between cash inflows and cash outflows, thus guaranteeing the solvency of the bank;
- To coordinate the issuing by the bank of short, medium and long term financing instruments;
- To optimise the costs of refinancing, striking a trade-off balance between liquidity and profitability;
- To optimise, for banks structured as banking groups, the intra-group management of cash flows, with the aim of reducing dependence on external financial requirements, by means of cash pooling techniques or other optimisation instruments.

The liquidity management processes and related risks vary depending on the size of the bank, the type of its main activity, the degree of internationalization and its organisational complexity. In all cases, however, such processes require to measure and control separately two liquidity dimensions[8]:

- The management of structural liquidity, often simply called liquidity management, aims to maintain, in the medium-long term, an adequate correspondence between monetary income and expenditure on different time horizons. It is evident that this structural capacity becomes, in principle, more difficult the larger is the maturity transformation implemented by the bank. If the average weighted duration of the assets is higher than that of the liabilities, the cash flows generated by the liquidation of the assets in a given period are lower than the cash flows needed for the payment of the liabilities in the very same time span. Such a situation highlights the potential liquidity risk borne by the bank as it strives to maintain a constant capacity for credit in the market; that is to say, the ability to renew matured liabilities—without prejudice to profitability—in order to link the expiry date of the liabilities with that of the assets;
- The management of short term liquidity, also known as treasury management, aims to ensure the capacity of the bank to deal with any expected and unexpected payment, emerging from contracts that put the bank in the position of

---

[8] Banks (2005).

facing a monetary outflow. The achievement of this goal depends on the availability of adequate cash reserves of liquid assets or eligibility for the central banks' refinancing, and all the instruments available to accommodate temporary imbalances between cash inflows and cash outflows.

Liquidity management is directed at achieving financial balance and aimed at guiding the operative interventions designed to influence the temporal order of cash flows. Through the management of liquidity, the bank's management outlines the boundaries and management criteria of the contingent components of assets, liabilities and off-balance sheet items over the medium to long term and the scope of work to be accomplished in the short term.

Structural liquidity management can be traced back to the convenience and the opportunity to change the qualitative and quantitative composition of assets, liabilities and off-balance sheet items, influencing the future and dynamic perspective of financial flows.

The definition of the broad management guidelines for the dynamics of assets, liabilities and off-balance sheet items in the medium and long term, which impact on the degree of structural liquidity, focuses on:

- The degree of maturity transformation that is considered acceptable;
- The bank's funding policy and the analysis of the bank's position in relation to the degree of closure of the deposit-lending financial circuit;
- The possible use of innovative forms of funding based on the transfer of part of the assets owned by the bank;
- The qualitative and quantitative components of the bank's asset composition policy and the assessment of the impact of the off-balance sheet items;
- The assessment of commercial policies that result in absorption of liquidity;
- The degree of the bank's risk appetite and the definition of methods to control liquidity risk.[9]

Short term liquidity management stems from the need to readily and economically accommodate imbalances between cash outflows and cash inflows, balancing immediate monetary dynamics. The setting of the operating margin for manoeuvring liquidity in the short and very short term is directed primarily at the rapid and effective arrangement of differences between cash outflows and inflows, and involves the identification of the contingent components on these time horizons. It relates specifically to:

- The determination of the volume and quality of highly liquid assets that can be liquidated in case of need or that can be used as collateral in refinancing operations;
- The identification of the range of treasury instruments to be activated in case of need;

---

[9] Murphy (2008).

- The setting of the degree of integration and intensity of the presence of the bank in the interbank market.[10]

The treasury management of the bank can then be conveniently represented as the sum of both reserves and liquid assets that are convertible into cash (bank reserves, respectively, of first and second line) and the set of procedures and instruments used to settle imbalances between cash outflows and cash inflows. This process of temporal allocation of cash flows is achieved by selecting different instruments and maturities available to allocate (if imbalance is positive) or to finance (if negative) the daily imbalance between outflows and inflows. The adjustment of the volume and composition of the first and second lines of liquidity reserves that go with it also involves an ongoing review of the asset-liability position and, therefore, the choices of convenience and economic exposure to interest rate risk and to liquidity risk.[11]

The economic analysis of liquidity risk can be carried out under six different headings:

1. The impact area of the liquidity risk,
2. The timeframe of the risk analysis,
3. The origin of the risk,
4. The economic scenario of the risk,
5. The models of risk measurement, and
6. The organisational processes and structures.

3.1 The Impact Area of the Liquidity Risk

Liquidity risk is caused by different constituent elements which are handled in different ways in each bank, according to its internal structure and to its respective risk appetite.

Depending on the possible impact area, however, the liquidity risk suffered by a bank falls into one of two intrinsically linked macro-categories: *funding liquidity risk* and *market liquidity risk*.[12]

Funding liquidity risk refers to the possibility that the bank may not be able to settle its obligations immediately and in a cost-effective way. It depends on expected and unexpected future cash inflows and outflows, linked to repayments of its liabilities, commitments to provide funds or requests to increase already provided guarantees.

Market liquidity risk, by contrast, is the risk which a bank may face when unable to convert a position on a given financial asset into money or when it has to

---

[10] Ruozi (2011).

[11] Adrian and Shin (2008), CEBS (2008).

[12] The Joint Forum (2006).

Table 1 The economic dimensions of liquidity risk

Economic dimension	Liquidity risk
Impact area	Funding liquidity risk
	Market liquidity risk
Timeframe	Short term liquidity risk
	Structural liquidity risk
Origin	Corporate liquidity risk
	Systemic liquidity risk
Economic scenario	Going concern liquidity risk
	Contingency liquidity risk

liquidate it and take a price cut, due to the insufficient market liquidity in which such an asset is negotiated, or to a temporary malfunctioning of the market itself.

In spite of the fact that they are distinct on a theoretical level, these two risk concepts are strictly linked to each other. The need to meet unexpected cash outflows could in fact force the bank to convert into money more or less substantial amounts of its financial assets. However, if this implies suffering potential losses, the damage arising from the liquidity risk will evidently be more pronounced.[13]

The recent changes in the international banking system have blurred the distinction between the two definitions of risk. The changeover from a model for the provision of originate-to-hold credit, in which the loan granted by the individual bank is maintained in the banking book right up to its repayment, to an originate-to-distribute model, in which the bank providing the loan arranges to transfer the risk to others by means of loan sale operations or, more frequently, securitisation, has increased the technical solution for liquidity risk management, allowing the conversion into cash of previously illiquid and non-tradable positions. At the same time, however, such changes have exposed banks to many more adverse market-contingent situations which make it no longer possible to liquidate items which could previously have been transferred to an appropriate vehicle, incorporated in financial instruments and surrendered to third parties in the markets. Arising from

---

[13] Banks (2005).

this, a stricter inter-ratio has emerged between the two concepts of liquidity risk defined above.[14]

The most commonly studied configuration of liquidity risk in the financial sector, on which most attention has been concentrated, is that of funding liquidity risk. This has an idiosyncratic character and can very quickly trigger reactions by market counterparts, which become unavailable for usual transactions or, on the other hand, demand a greater counterparty payment. The effects of both circumstances, jointly, can reverberate on the solvency situation of a bank which is experiencing liquidity stress.

Market liquidity risk, because of the strict inter-ratio with market risks, was often measured and managed by the risk management unit entrusted with the valuation of market risks, instead of the unit set up for the measurement and management of liquidity risk.[15] It should be noted that, until a short time ago, this risk was completely ignored by the risk management systems of banks in the leading industrialised countries.[16]

3.2 The Timeframe of the Risk Analysis

The processes of management and the methods for measuring liquidity risk vary according to the size of the bank, its prevalent type of assets, its level of internationalization, and its relative organisational complexity.

In all events, however, such processes attempt to measure and to monitor separately:

- The management of short term liquidity, whose aim is to guarantee the ability to meet in the immediate future any repayment commitment, foreseen or unforeseen, arising from contracts which place the bank in the position of having to carry out a monetary act. This ability depends on the availability of adequate liquidity buffers, consisting of cash and other highly liquid unencumbered assets, and on refinancing facilities available to face temporary imbalances between incoming and outgoing cash flows[17];
- The management of structural liquidity, whose aim is to maintain in the medium-long term an adequate balance between monetary inflows and outflows over different time horizons. It is evident that this structural ability becomes even more challenging the bigger the maturity transformation is in the banking book.

---

[14] For more detail on the so-called "liquidity spirals" that involve a closer interrelationship between funding liquidity risk and market liquidity risk, see: Garleanu and Pedersen (2007), Brunnermeier and Pedersen (2009), CEBS (2008).

[15] Deutsche Bundesbank and Bafin (2008).

[16] Bangia et al. (2001), Bervas (2006).

[17] Matz and Neu (2007).

While the problems of short term liquidity management (*short term liquidity risk*) arise from the need to promptly and economically fix the imbalances between cash inflows and outflows, thus immediately re-establishing monetary dynamics, the problems of structural liquidity management (*structural liquidity risk*) can be handled conveniently and opportunely by modifying the qualitative-quantitative composition of assets, liabilities and off-balance sheet items, in affecting the future and dynamic perspective of cash flows.

In reality, the two aspects of liquidity management are strictly linked and mutually condition each other.

The most convincing and comprehensive explanation of the latter statement can be found in the recent banking crises that have characterised various national and international contexts. They have resulted in a liquidity crisis caused by structural problems that have spilled over into the management of the short term, in fact making it unmanageable. This is precisely the crisis situation that highlights the relationship between short term liquidity and structural liquidity, especially when it is sufficiently intense to create difficulties for the bank, triggering liquidity problems which are no longer manageable, but which are not attributable solely to the liquidity management and to those responsible for it, but were instead fueled by decisions taken upstream.

The liquidity crisis is almost always the result and not the cause of the recent banking crises. At the origin of these problems there has been a departure from the principles of sound and prudent management that banking doctrine identified a long time ago, and an excessive orientation towards achieving short term profits, combined with the ineffectiveness of banks' internal control systems and, in some countries, the inadequate policies of the supervisory authorities.

This has resulted in the evolution of a style of liquidity management that was characterised by a strong imbalance between inflows and outflows, which it was no longer possible to keep within physiological limits. The old and established principle of banking doctrine, for which an instantaneous and continuous equilibrium between cash inflows and outflows in the medium-long term can be expected only where there is an equilibrium between the structures for assets and liabilities maturity dates, has often been overlooked.

In summary, structural liquidity management should hinge on more general management of the bank and, in particular, on all funding and lending operations and on all the costs and revenues that generate cash flows.

3.3 The Origin of the Risk

Liquidity risk is in some measure intrinsic to the banking business. Nevertheless, there exist some elements which can accentuate the exposure of a bank to liquidity risk: technical factors, factors specific to an individual bank, and factors of a systemic nature.

The development of financial instruments with complex timely cash flow structures, the wide contingent nature of many instruments, be it in funding or lending, the extensive recourse to types of liquidity enhancement in securitisation operations, or the development of payment systems which operate in real time and on a multilateral basis, all determine the increase of liquidity risk, especially for the larger banks which are more exposed to risk due to their multi-currency transnational operations across time zones which generally characterise such operations.

Over and above these technical elements, there can also be factors specific to the bank which, with weakening public or operational trust, can exacerbate the liquidity risk in determining a funding difficulty. There are examples of this: downgrading phenomena or other events, also of a reputational type, responsible for damage to the bank's image or a loss of public trust; phenomena connected to the specific nature of some financial instruments with margin mechanisms and guarantee management. All of these could give rise to an unforeseen liquidity requirement were particularly volatile markets to be present; phenomena linked to the so-called commitments to provide funds and other undrawn off-balance sheet positions, which in certain market situations can generate an extraordinary liquidity requirement.

In short, the presence of systemic factors can cause generalised funding problems for different banks and potential difficulties with financial asset disinvestment: these are independent situational events for the individual bank and events linked to crises in the financial markets, economic-political crises, natural catastrophes, acts of terrorism, etc.[18]

The occurrence of all these elements, whether singly or jointly, generates a liquidity risk linked to internal bank factors (*corporate liquidity risk*) and a risk linked to market factors or systemic factors outside the control of the bank (*systemic liquidity risk*).

3.4 The Economic Scenario of the Risk

According to the economic scenario in which the bank finds itself, it is possible to distinguish the liquidity risk dealt with in the course of normal operations—*going concern liquidity risk*—and the risk dealt with in stress situations—*contingency liquidity risk*—both of which are linked to individual or systemic factors.

In the first case, the risk is connected to situations in which the bank is in a position of meeting its own liquidity requirement using its own funding ability. In a going concern scenario, liquidity management and the correct measurement of related risks presuppose the simulation of the evolution of cash inflows and

---

[18] Murphy (2008).

outflows, in adopting the most neutral possible hypotheses with respect to the evolution of on- and off-balance sheet items.

In the second case, the risk is met in stressed conditions which derive from either individual or systemic factors. As such crises cannot be met by means of the normal funding ability of the bank, it becomes necessary to have recourse to ex ante formalised extraordinary measures by means of a prior drawing up of an appropriate contingency funding plan. Such a document formalises the intervention strategy, lists the possible types of liquidity stress, identifying the systemic or specific nature of each tension and the balance sheet items most affected, identifies the emergency action to be taken by management and contains the estimates of back-up liquidity at the disposal of the bank in order to face a liquidity crisis (Table 1).[19]

3.5 Models and Measurement Techniques

From the technical point of view, the measurement of liquidity risk needs to distinguish between the two macro-categories of funding liquidity risk and that of market liquidity risk.[20]

3.5.1 The Funding Liquidity Risk

In the case of funding liquidity risk, there are still no robust and jointly shared management methodologies and the matter is handled in different ways in various countries. However, the most widespread models for measuring such risk are to be found in one of the following three categories (Table 2):

- Stock-based approaches,
- Cash flow matching approaches, and
- Hybrid approaches.

Stock-Based Approaches

Stock-based approaches measure the volume of financial assets, which can be speedily liquidated or used in refinancing facilities, of which the bank can dispose to meet a future liquidity crisis. In essence, by means of these models, the

---

[19] Banque de France (2008).

[20] The Joint Forum (2006).

Table 2 The measurement models of funding liquidity risk

Approaches	Assumptions	Indicators	Merits	Shortcomings
Stock-based approaches	By comparing balance sheet items, stock-based approaches aim to determine the ability of a bank to cover its liquidity needs by measuring the amount of liquid assets that can be promptly liquidated or used to obtain secured loans	Cash capital position Long term funding ratios	Indicators are easy to calculate These approaches facilitate the assessment of the vulnerability of a bank to a sudden liquidity shortage	These approaches provide a static representation of liquidity risk, neglecting the amount and the timing of cash inflows and outflows
Cash flow-based (or mismatch-based) approaches	The cash flow approaches are based on maturity ladders used to compare the bank's future cash inflows and cash outflows over a series of specified timeframes. The aim is to measure a cash flow mismatch	Cash flow gaps	These approaches offer a dynamic representation of liquidity risk	Indicators are more difficult to calculate These approaches complicate the assessment of the vulnerability of a bank to a sudden liquidity shortage
Hybrid approaches	Hybrid approaches combine elements of the stock-based approaches and cash flows matching	Liquidity mismatches between cash inflows and cash outflows integrated by the stock of unencumbered assets usable to generate cash inflows	These approaches are able to integrate the advantages of the two previous categories of models	These approaches are able to partially overcome the limitations of the two previous categories of models

vulnerability of a bank to liquidity risk is quantified by means of simple indicators based on the amount, quality and nature of the bank's stock of assets.[21]

The two main indicators are the cash capital position and the medium-long term funding ratios.

The cash capital position is obtained by subtracting from unencumbered assets that can be easily or immediately liquidated by the bank, liabilities that are repayable on demand or that have a very short term whose renewal cannot be considered reasonably certain, and the commitment to supply funds which carry with them an irrevocable obligation to grant cash sums to customers:

$$\text{Cash capital position} = \text{Unencumbered assets} - \text{Short term interbank funding}$$
$$- \text{Noncore deposits} - \text{Undrawn commitments}$$

The medium-long term funding ratios are measured by means of the ratio between the liabilities with a medium-to-long maturity date and the assets which have an at least linked duration:

$$\text{Long-term funding ratio} = \frac{\text{Sum of available funding maturing above "n" years}}{\text{Sum of assets maturing above "n" years}}$$

By virtue of the maturity transformation function operated by banks, it is normal to expect that long-term funding ratios will frequently be less than 100 %. However, the drop of one or more ratios below certain limits can be interpreted as an indicator of the bank's vulnerability to liquidity risk.

These indicators provide accordingly a representation of a static type of liquidity risk, in that they ignore the dynamics of financial inflows and outflows connected with the entire bank management and the exact moment in which they become manifest.

Cash Flow Matching Approaches

A more satisfying approximation to reality demands a shift from a static analysis, based on a comparison with stock of assets, to a dynamic analysis, in which the liquidity situation is assessed by generated or absorbed financial flows in a given timeframe. Mismatch-based approaches respond to such an aim by identifying future cash inflows and outflows, grouping them in homogeneous maturity date bundles, and verifying the presence of an adequate balance between the former and the latter. The application of such models presupposes that the different future cash flows are subdivided, by means of a series of maturity ladders, with the aim of establishing the balance between the cash inflows and outflows in differently referenced timeframes.[22]

---

[21] Resti and Sironi (2007).

[22] Matz and Neu (2007).

These maturity ladders make it possible to measure the balance between expected cash inflows and expected cash outflows in each time band and, through the construction of cumulative balances, reach the net financial position on successive time horizons. In this regard, each bank will have to address the methodological options related to defining the time horizon of reference, modelling off-balance sheet cash flows and those characterised by a contingent nature in the use or reimbursement from customers.

Normally, the creation of two categories of maturity ladders is arranged as follows:

• The first, tactical or operational maturity ladders, aimed at the short term;
• The other, strategic maturity ladders, aimed at the long term.

The distinction is based not only on the moment when flows become manifest, but also on the hypotheses which produce the definition of the volume and the timing of the flows in the two matrices. For flows relative to contingent components, the measurement used is based on stochastic or behavioural models, which differ according to the timeframe being considered.

A positive net flow, in a given period, measures the amount of financial resources which are going to be added to the existing ones and which can be reutilised in new activities.

A negative net flow indicates a requirement to find the resources that management needs in the given time span to cover the imbalance.

Hybrid Approaches

Hybrid approaches integrate the two preceding categories: in effect, to expected future net flows are added the inflows which could be obtained by using the stock of financial assets that can be liquidated easily and immediately or used as collateral in refinancing operations.[23]

At a first level, liquidity management based on hybrid models presupposes a simulated evolution of the balance between cash inflows and outflows in successive timeframes, exactly as it is done in cash flow matching approaches.

At a second level, the monitoring of the short term liquidity position envisages the measurement of the financial assets that can be promptly liquidated or committed in refinancing operations, including all positions capable of being refinanced with the central bank or that can be used as collateral in secured finance operations, by valuing them at market prices and applying the haircut required by the supervisory authority or by the bank's internal risk policy. The cumulative sum of net flows and of financial assets identifies the magnitude of the liquidity risk, which in normal conditions will have to be met.

---

[23] European Central Bank (2007).

At a third level, it is necessary to define the operating limits based on the definition of the maximum tolerable liquidity deficit as regards the different operational currencies and, also, within each unit of the banking group. The constant monitoring of such operating limits allows the preventive identification of the rise of potential liquidity crises implicit in the expected cash flows.[24]

Within these operating limits, the "cash horizon" indicator is becoming widely used. This metric is monitored through the short term maturity ladder and identifies the number of days after which the bank will no longer be able to meet its liquidity requirements, as represented in the tactical maturity ladder, once the available counterbalancing capacity has been completely used. The counterbalancing capacity represents the outstanding amount of highly liquid financial assets that can be sold or are eligible for refinancing operations, including all refinancing positions at the central bank or that can otherwise be used as collateral in secured finance transactions. In other words, the "cash horizon" represents the breakeven point between the cumulative gap positions that originate from cash flows and the stock of net financial assets eligible as collateral in secured finance transactions.

Technical Aspects

The application of all three category models presupposes the adjustment of contractual cash flows to derive the actual ones that correctly take into account possible alternative scenarios. Such adjustments vary according to whether the reference taken is a normal operation scenario or a stress scenario linked to individual or systemic factors.

In a scenario of normal operation, it is essential to identify all expected future cash flows arising from on- and off-balance sheet items and arrive at an estimation of the unexpected cash flows. On some items, the identification of expected future cash flows is relatively simple both in its amount and the timing of receipts and payments. On other operations incorporating a contingent nature, the prediction of future cash flows is complicated in relation to the timing of the event and/or the relevant amount. In this second case, the estimate of future cash flows requires the adoption of certain assumptions and the use of probabilistic or behavioural models that are able to predict with sufficient reliability the quantum and timing of future cash flows.

In a stressed scenario, simulation exercises are carried out to estimate the effects on the liquidity risk of particularly adverse situations. Input for carrying out such simulations can be taken from:

- Historical events that have involved the bank itself or its competitors (historical approach);
- Statistical simulation obtained from the distribution hypothesis of risk factors (statistical approach), or

---

[24] Banks (2005).

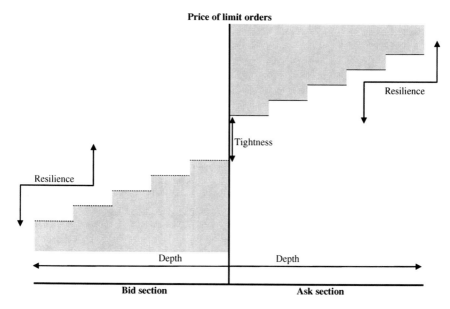

Fig. 2 Exogenous factors influencing market liquidity

- Subjective estimates formulated by the bank's management (judgement-based approach).[25]

  Such approaches can be used to simulate separately the effect of single risk factors or indeed to construct worst-case scenarios in which many factors act jointly, creating a potent liquidity stress on the bank or on the entire banking system.[26]

  Stress tests represent a relevant component in the measurement of liquidity risk, though their development is still at an experimental stage. Methodologies are still rather heterogeneous and often based on judgemental approaches both in reference to sensitivity analysis and in relation to scenario testing. Despite limits linked to the arbitrary nature of the data used, such simulations are useful in that they allow the bank to arrange in advance a contingency funding plan to be brought into play in the event that the adverse hypothesised scenarios occur.

3.5.2 The Market Liquidity Risk

In the case of market liquidity risk, risk measurement needs to consider the liquidity of the market in which the financial product is negotiable.

---

[25] Matz (2007).

[26] Resti and Sironi (2007).

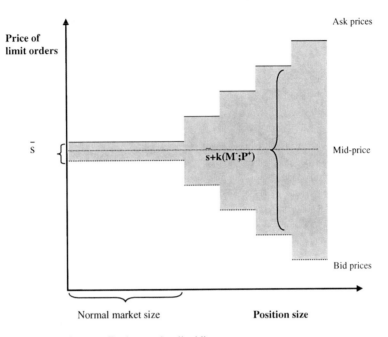

Fig. 3 Endogenous factors affecting market liquidity

In general, the liquidity of any financial instrument market depends on a multiplicity of factors:

- The rapidity with which a negotiation proposal can be executed;
- The implicit cost of the transaction in terms of the bid-ask spread;
- The ability to absorb immediately or quickly possible imbalances between bid- and offer-prices without creating sensitive price variations.

Theoretically, in a perfectly liquid market, it is possible to disinvest, with certainty in the shortest of times and at a single price, a position of any amount. In practice, the time and cost of disinvesting a position are relative to both exogenous and endogenous factors.[27]

Exogenous factors are the result of market liquidity characteristics and involve all potential participants.

They can be summarised in the depth, the spread between bid- and ask-prices, the resilience, and the immediacy of the market.[28] The *depth* of the market refers to its own capacity to absorb large trade volumes without a significant impact on the price. *Tightness* indicates the general cost incurred in a transaction irrespective of market price and is linked mainly, though not exclusively, to market spread. *Resilience* is the market's capacity to have new purchase and sale proposal flows to

[27] Bangia et al. (2001).

[28] International Monetary Fund (2006), Bervas (2006).

match a temporary imbalance between supply and demand. Finally, *immediacy* indicates the time that intervenes between dispatching the negotiation proposal and the completion of the transaction.

The joint operation of these factors determines the time and cost of disinvestment of a given position for any market participant (Fig. 2).[29]

Endogenous factors, on the contrary, are specific to some positions. They are related to the amount of the exposure and they grow with the increase of the position held, involving only some of the market participants.

Both types of factor must be integrated in the classical metrics of risk valuation in order to avoid the risk exposure of the bank being undervalued due to the market liquidity component and due to possible risks connected with the disinvestment of more or less substantial positions, necessary to meet any misalignment between cash inflows and outflows.[30]

Since, in general, banks evaluate their securities at the average price between bid and ask prices, when they proceed with the liquidation of a position, it is necessary to take into account the lower income related to the difference between average price and bid price, computing a cost that is equal to:

$$C = P \cdot \frac{s}{2}$$

where C is the cost borne, P is the price of the security under liquidation and s is the bid-ask spread expressed as a percentage.

As shown in Fig. 3, when the amount of the position held is significant, the actual spread may diverge significantly from its average value in normal market conditions ($\bar{s}$) and be much higher. This divergence is precisely linked to both exogenous factors, summarized in the overall market size (M), and endogenous factors, which are linked to the amount of the position that the bank intends to dispose of (P).

The total cost of market liquidity risk, therefore, becomes:

$$C = P \cdot \frac{[\bar{s} + k(M^-; P^+)]}{2}$$

where the average spread has to be increased by a factor k that is negatively related to overall market size (M) and positively related to the amount outstanding of the position held (P).

Identifying the function that links the factor k to the overall market size and to the amount of the position held is far from simple. Several researchers have tried to explain this feature, by inserting additional factors that can better represent the overall size of the spread and they should be consulted for a discussion of the topic.[31]

---

[29] Borio (2000).

[30] Bervas (2006).

[31] Bangia et al. (2001), Jarrow and Protter (2005), Amihud et al. (2005), Angelidis and Benos (2006), Stange and Kaserer (2008).

3.6 Organisational Processes and Structures

From the organisational point of view, the units charged for the management of liquidity risk perform the following functions:

- Measurement of liquidity risk,
- Development and adoption of management models,
- Carrying out of stress tests,
- Verification of compliance with various indicators where subject to limits,
- Provision of daily information to top management,
- Establishing a system of liquidity early warning indicators that is needed to monitor on an ongoing basis any stressful situations, and
- Development of a contingency funding plan in the event of a liquidity crisis.[32]

At times, the same organisational units also accomplish some additional functions such as:

- Fixing of internal prices for liquidity transfer,
- Definition of hedge plans to meet financial requirements, identifying the most opportune maturity dates of the various traditional and innovative manners of funding, and
- Approval of liquidity transfers between various banks within the group.

A survey conducted on the European banking system shows the liquidity risk management procedures within the major banking groups.[33] From such a survey, it emerges that the measurement of liquidity risk, operating limits, medium-long term management guidelines, and the contingency funding plan in the majority of observed cases is centralised by the parent bank. The margins of operational manoeuvrability in the short and very short term are, in some cases, fixed on the basis of complete centralisation in the parent bank. In other cases of complete decentralisation, the parent bank limits itself to setting down principles for the measurement and control of liquidity risk, but short term operational management is entirely consigned to the individual banks comprising part of the group (Fig. 4).[34]

Centralised management models for short term liquidity are typically adopted in banking groups which operate at a national level with a rather homogeneous banking model. These presume:

- The pooling of liquidity cash flows at an individual entity of the group, typically the parent bank,

---

[32] CEBS (2007).

[33] European Central Bank (2007).

[34] This refers specifically to "banking groups" since the presence of foreign direct branches, rather than the presence of local companies, is always associated with a centralised model. CEBS (2007).

Centralised models	Coordinated models	Decentralised models
The fully centralised model concentrates funding and liquidity management at the central treasury at the group level which distributes funding around a bank's branches and subsidiaries, monitors compliance with centrally mandated mismatch limits and meets centrally any shortfalls. In this model: - The parent company defines the framework, limits and funding instructions; - Subsidiaries implement policies as instructed.	In the coordinated model there are liquidity centres which are legal entities that act in their responsibility as a liquidity hub and which are in charge of the liquidity management and concentration process of liquidity flows of the subsidiaries falling within their perimeter of responsibility. The liquidity centres are in charge of the funding optimization carried out on the relevant local markets and are responsible for coordinating the access to short term and medium-to-long term markets of the legal entities within their perimeter. Finally, liquidity centres are also in charge of the implementation of the group's liquidity rules. In this model: - The parent company defines the framework, guidelines and limits with a focus on the main currencies, wholesale and long term funding; - Subsidiaries focus on other currencies, retail and short term funding and implement somewhat flexibly policies on the main currencies.	The fully decentralised model devolves the responsibility for funding and liquidity management to the individual local entities, which act as a collection of autonomous banks under common ownership. The bank's branches and subsidiaries source funding in host countries and meet any shortfalls autonomously. In this model: - At the parent company level, a group assets and liabilities committee (ALCO) defines strategies, policies, methodologies, limits and approves local ALCOs' decisions; - Local ALCOs define their policies within the boundaries set by the Group ALCO.

Fig. 4 The alternative organisational models for liquidity management. *Source* Based on ECB (2007), CGFS (2010)

- A single access to money markets, and
- A single access to refinancing channels at the central bank.

The main advantages of the centralised model are: the optimisation of funding costs thanks to the logic of cash pooling; control of the liquidity position of the individual banks; greater attention to counterparty risk on the money markets and stricter monitoring of liquidity risk generally borne at group level. On the other hand, by means of such a model, a greater managerial sophistication is created, due to the logic of pooling, and the risks of contagion are increased in times of crisis.

Decentralised managerial models for short term liquidity risk are more wide-spread within global banks that are characterised by multi-country, multi-currency operations and over more time zones. In this instance, the model presupposes:

- Individual and autonomous management of liquidity by each bank belonging to the banking group, with due regard for the guidelines set down by the parent bank,
- Access by the individual bank within the group either to the money markets or to refinancing at the central bank.

If, on the one hand, such a model carries the merit of less managerial sophistication and a reduction in the risks of 'contagion' in the event of crises, on the other hand, it does not optimise the costs of funding, due to the possible internal non-compensation of opposing cash flows, and it reduces the depth of the liquidity risk analysis borne by each individual unit of the banking group. Nevertheless, such a model has the merit of making each individual bank in the group responsible for the liquidity risk, which avoids the parent bank being considered a sort of lender of last resort in the event of erroneous managerial policies from which misalignments between cash inflows and outflows may result. At a European level, more than two thirds of the larger banking groups with transnational operations are seen to have adopted this model, as shown by an analysis carried out by the European Central Bank.[35]

The two models described above represent the extremes of a continuum within which each individual banking group can adopt intermediate configurations based on a semi-centralised multi-hub type model. Here the centralisation of liquidity management occurs at a level of two or more banks within the group, which operate as 'access points' to the money markets and to refinancing channels, and carry out a balancing of the liquidity surplus or deficit over a certain geographical area and, often, for a given currency. Such intermediate models are employed especially by banks that operate in many markets, in different banking areas and with high volumes, and using them aims to combine the merits of the two previous models.[36]

Whatever the organisational model, each bank must provide for the development of two key documents:

---

[35] European Central Bank (2007).

[36] CGFS (2010).

- The liquidity funding plan;
- The contingency funding plan.

The liquidity funding plan plays a fundamental role in the overall management of the liquidity position of the bank, influencing both the short term and the structural liquidity position. This document sets out the funding strategies of the bank in line with the budgeting process, the development and investment objectives, the market situation and the funding procedures available to the bank.[37]

The liquidity funding plan should be developed having the degree of risk appetite of the bank as a constraint, and the optimization of the cost of funding as an aim.

Risk appetite, typically formalized by quantitative indicators and monitored through appropriate means of control, must be defined by the board of directors and must be consistent with the requirements of prudential supervision and the structural and functional characteristics of the bank.

The optimization of the cost of funding must be compatible with the bank's need to remain in a position to meet its payment obligations in the event of a liquidity crisis. This optimization process must comply with laws and regulations and internal policies and rules.

Instead, the contingency funding plan has the aim of protecting the bank in a liquidity crisis, by means of a prior preventive arrangement and a successive implementation of crisis management strategies and procedures for finding sources of financing in the event of an emergency, by defining the competences of the various banking units in such situations.

A contingency funding plan considers future cash flow projections, both inflows and outflows, under alternative scenarios concerning on- and off-balance sheet items and liquidity risk mitigation tools. Such scenarios can be sub-divided into three categories:

- A going concern scenario, in which the liquidity stresses experienced by the bank are not acute and are regulated by countermeasures which fall within ordinary management;
- An acutely stressed liquidity at the level of an individual bank, which frequently entails recourse to extraordinary countermeasures and external intervention for the bank;
- A crisis scenario for the entire market.

The contingency funding plan identifies the different sources from which a bank can draw in the event of a liquidity crisis, the priority in which such sources should be accessed, the banking entities and competent structures for putting into effect extraordinary funding policies in case of need. The contingency funding plan is not only a response to a liquidity crisis, but in turn, in a way, also determines its breadth and final exit.[38]

---

[37] CGFS (2010).
[38] Deutsche Bundesbank (2008).

4 Liquidity Risk: Regulatory Issues

Even before the explosive crisis of the summer of 2007, various international organisations widely analysed the causes and the procedures of liquidity risk management. However, they failed to envisage fixing a common set of procedures which up to the present time has been left to the discretion of the individual national supervisory authorities.

The first international Basel Accord on bank capital in 1988 did not even mention the liquidity risk borne by the banks and only in 1992 did the Basel Committee on Banking Supervision (BCBS) pose the problem of ensuring minimum management standards for such a risk with the major international banks and only limited itself to disseminating a report containing the most appropriate measurement and management principles.[39] This document was subsequently updated in 2000, aligning the principles of liquidity risk management with developments taking place in the meantime in major international banks' practices.[40] Yet this document too, though listing 14 principles of correct liquidity risk management, had a purely informative value and did not constitute an amendment to the 1988 Basel Accord on bank capital.

In 2006, the Joint Forum—composed by BCBS, the International Organization of Securities Commissions (IOSCO) and the International Association of Insurance Supervisors (IAIS)—published a report entitled 'The Management of Liquidity Risk in Financial Groups', in which the problem of the management of liquidity risk was analysed at the level of financial groups with a prevalent banking, insurance or securities brokerage activity. In this case too, the document had value in sharing best international practices, but did not dictate guidelines for incorporation into the national regulations of the leading industrialized countries.[41]

Up to the recent financial crisis, at international level there has been a broad consensus on the fact that liquidity risk must not be covered by specific capital requirements, since it does not directly affect the area of profitability. A peculiarity of liquidity risk—at least in its meaning of funding liquidity risk—which distinguishes it from other risks is that it manifests itself by means of temporary imbalances between monetary inflows and outflows which do not necessarily result in losses. A bank that is facing an unexpected cash requirement can overcome it without a particularly extraordinary economic burden. Precisely because of this, the imbalances between cash inflows and outflows, and the consequent liquidity risk, need to be covered not by means of capital paid in by shareholders—unlike credit, market and operational risks—but rather by maintaining an adequate volume of liquid buffers and by activating the monitoring processes and operating systems which make it possible to meet a sudden liquidity deficit.

---

[39] Basel Committee on Banking Supervision (1992).

[40] Basel Committee on Banking Supervision (2000).

[41] The Joint Forum (2006).

Coherent with such a vision, Basel II has not contemplated liquidity risk within the minimum capital requirements which constitute 'Pillar one' of the international accord. It was therefore envisaged, within the internal capital adequacy assessment process known as 'Pillar two', that every bank should adopt adequate systems to measure, monitor and control liquidity risk.

'Pillar two', known as the supervisory review process, is divided into two phases that integrate each other:

- The internal capital adequacy assessment process (or ICAAP), with which banks must make an independent assessment of capital adequacy, present and future, in relation to the risks assumed and to corporate strategy. The calculation of total internal capital requires a thorough assessment of all risks to which banks are or may be exposed, both those considered in the calculation of capital requirements and those which are not considered as liquidity risk;[42]
- The supervisory review and evaluation process (or SREP), with which the supervisor analyses the process of internal control, assesses the consistency of the results, gives an overall judgment and adopts, where necessary, corrective measures.

As liquidity is an essential condition for the operating continuity of any bank, Basel II required the adequacy of capital to be valued in the light of the liquidity profile of the bank and of the market liquidity in which the bank operates. Within 'Pillar three', based on market discipline and bank transparency, Basel II envisaged that, for each risk area, the bank has to describe corporate strategies, objectives and practices, managing techniques and methods, signalling systems, hedging policies and/or risk mitigation. However, it did not request specific information in relation to liquidity risk and left to the national supervisory authorities the task of deciding whether to force the bank to divulge to the markets information on this type of risk.[43]

However, Basel III has introduced—as well as new rules on capital, leverage, interaction between prudential rules and the economic cycle, and the operation of banks in structured finance—harmonized international minimum requirements based on a one-size-fits-all approach, without taking into account the specificities of each bank's business model and the structural and functional characteristics of each banking system. The new regulatory framework has developed global liquidity standards and supervisory monitoring procedures based on three categories of tools:

- Common principles for sound liquidity management and supervision;
- Minimum standards of liquidity;
- Monitoring tools to assess liquidity risk.

---

[42] The ICAAP can be decomposed into the following phases: (1) identification of risks to be evaluated, (2) measurement and evaluation of individual risks and the internal capital needed to meet them, (3) measurement of total internal capital in relation to the totality of risks borne, and (4) determining the total capital and reconciliation with the regulatory capital.

[43] Basel Committee on Banking Supervision (2006).

The objective of these three categories of tools is to raise banks' resilience to the liquidity stress that can occur both in normal operating circumstances characterised by a stable market situation, and in stressed scenarios, with liquidity shortage at the bank level or at systemic level.

4.1 Common Principles for Sound Liquidity Management and Supervision

In 2008, the BCBS conducted a survey on the approaches adopted by the individual national supervisory authorities on the subject of liquidity risk management and updated its previous 2000 document containing the principles for sound liquidity risk management and supervision. In this report, it confirmed that the management of liquidity risk does not demand a capital requirement, but must be met by means of sound internal procedures that provide adequate systems of control over the liquidity risk management processes, including regular independent reviews and evaluations of the effectiveness of these systems.[44] The recent international crisis has in fact shown how well capitalised banks can also meet temporary liquidity crises: even if higher levels of capital provide public trust in the market participants, they are not sufficient to avoid liquidity problems, which can be prevented only by sound internal systems and effective operating limits.[45]

Liquidity risk management aims at achieving a financial equilibrium and is directed at guiding the operative interventions designed to influence the order of temporal flows. Through the management of liquidity, the bank's managers identify the boundaries and management criteria for the future dynamics of assets, liabilities and off-balance sheet items over the medium to long term and the scope of work to be accomplished in the short term.[46]

The principles point out the importance of establishing a robust liquidity risk management and supervision framework and seek to improve standards in the following areas:

- Identification and measurement of the full range of liquidity risks, including contingent liquidity risks;
- Definition of a bank-wide liquidity risk tolerance;
- Maintenance of an adequate level of liquidity, including through a cushion of unencumbered high-quality liquid assets;
- Need to allocate liquidity costs, benefits and risks to all significant business units, also through the setting of internal prices;

---

[44] Basel Committee on Banking Supervision (2008).

[45] Among other studies on the management of liquidity risk particularly noteworthy is: Persaud (2003); IIF (2007); Senior Supervisors Group (2009).

[46] Nikolaou (2009).

- Design and use of severe stress-test scenarios aimed at estimating the effects on liquidity risk of adverse situations;
- Need for a robust and operational contingency funding plan, aimed at protecting the bank in a crisis of liquidity by the prior preparation and subsequent implementation of strategies and crisis management procedures for the collection of sources of funding in case of emergency, defining the responsibilities of the various governing bodies in these situations;
- Careful management of risks relating to intraday liquidity risk and collateral positions;
- Regular public disclosure on how the bank measures and manages liquidity risk to promote market discipline.

These principles provide the cornerstone of a robust liquidity risk management framework and, together with minimum liquidity standards and monitoring tools, also strengthen the role of supervisors to intervene in a timely manner to address deficiencies, both within and across national borders.

4.2 Minimum Liquidity Standards

To complement these principles of sound and prudent management, the BCBS has further strengthened the regulatory framework by introducing two minimum coefficients of liquidity: the liquidity coverage ratio and the net stable funding ratio. These standards have been developed to reach two separate but complementary objectives. The first is to measure the vulnerability of a bank to a liquidity crisis in a very short time (30 days), ensuring that it has sufficient unencumbered, high-quality liquid assets to survive an acute phase of cash outflows, associated with a stressed macroeconomic and operating scenario. The second is to prevent potential imbalances in the structure for maturities of assets and liabilities, strengthening the incentives for a bank to finance its activities with more stable sources of funding on an ongoing structural basis.[47]

4.2.1 The Liquidity Coverage Ratio

The liquidity coverage ratio (LCR) requires a bank to have sufficient high-quality liquid assets to withstand a 30-day stressed funding scenario with significant, but not catastrophic tensions. Such scenarios include: a downgrade of the credit rating of the bank by up to three notches; the withdrawal of a portion of non-maturity deposits; a reduction of unsecured wholesale funding; a significant increase in the haircut applied in secured finance operations; an increase in margin requirements on derivatives positions; significant payment claims against off-balance sheet

---

[47] Bini Smaghi (2010).

exposures; the potential need for the bank to buy back its debt or to honour contractual obligations to mitigate the reputational risk.[48]

This standard [aims] to ensure that a bank maintains an adequate level of unencumbered, high-quality liquid assets that can be converted into cash to meet its liquidity needs under a significantly severe liquidity stress scenario lasting 30 days.

The standard requires that the value of high-quality liquid assets should at least equal the total net cash outflows, i.e., the value of the ratio should be no lower than 1:

$$\text{LCR} = \frac{\text{stock of high-quality liquid assets}}{\text{total net cash outflows}} \geq 1$$

Under the liquidity coverage standard, a bank must hold a stock of unencumbered high-quality liquid assets to fill funding gaps between cash outflows and cash inflows over a 30-day stress period and as a defence against the potential onset of severe liquidity stress.

In order to be included in high-quality liquid assets, instruments should be easily and immediately converted into cash at little or no loss of value and, ideally, be eligible for central banks' standing facilities. The main features of high-quality liquid assets are: low market and credit risk, ease and certainty of valuation, low correlation with risky assets and listing on a recognized market. These characteristics ensure that they can be converted into cash even in conditions of idiosyncratic and market stress.

The stock of high-quality liquid assets held by a bank is obtained by multiplying on-balance sheet accounting values by a factor set at international level, taking into account the quality of each category of assets. There are two categories of assets that can be included in the amount of high-quality liquid assets:

- "Level 1" assets can be included without limit and qualify for a 100 % factor. These assets include cash, qualifying central bank reserves, qualifying marketable securities from sovereigns, central banks, public sector entities and multilateral development banks, domestic sovereign or central bank debt securities in domestic currency and also in foreign currency to the extent they match bank liquidity needs in that jurisdiction;
- "Level 2" assets can only comprise up to 40 % of the stock and qualify for an 85 % factor (equivalent to a haircut of 15 %) to take into account their lower liquidity. These assets embrace: sovereign, central bank and public sector entities assets qualifying for 20 % risk weighting under Basel II standardised approach, qualifying corporate bonds rated AA- or higher, qualifying covered bonds rated AA- or higher (Table 3).

Total net cash outflows refer to the total expected cash outflows for the subsequent 30-days minus the total expected cash inflows over the same period up to,

---

[48] Basel Committee on Banking Supervision (2010).

Table 3 High-quality liquid assets categories

Category	Factor (%)
Level 1 assets	
Cash	100
Central bank reserves to the extent that they can be drawn down under stress	100
Marketable securities from sovereigns, central banks, public sector entities and multilateral development banks traded in large and deep markets, able to provide liquidity even in stressed market conditions, and qualifying for a 0 % risk-weight under Basel II standardised approach	100
Domestic sovereign or central bank debt securities issued in domestic currency even if risk-weight under Basel II standardised approach is higher than 0 %	100
Domestic sovereign or central bank debt securities issued in foreign currency even if risk-weight under Basel II standardised approach is higher than 0 % to the extent that currency matches bank's liquidity needs in jurisdiction of issue	100
Level 2 assets[a]	
Marketable securities from sovereign, central bank and public sector entities assets traded in large and deep markets, able to provide liquidity even in stressed market conditions, and qualifying for 20 % risk-weight under Basel II standardised approach	85
Corporate bonds rated AA- or higher, traded in large and deep markets, able to provide liquidity even in stressed market conditions, not issued by financial institutions of their affiliated entities	85
Covered bonds rated AA- or higher, traded in large and deep markets, able to provide liquidity even in stressed market conditions, not issued by the bank itself or its affiliated entities	85

[a] Subject to a cap of 40 % of the total amount of high-quality liquid assets
Source Based on Basel Committee on Banking Supervision (2010)

as we will see, an aggregate cap of 75 % of total expected cash outflows, in the specified stress scenario:

$$Total\, net\, cash\, outflows = outflows - min\, \{inflows;\ 75\,\%\ of\, outflows\}$$

Total expected cash outflows are calculated by multiplying the outstanding aggregates of on- and off-balance sheet commitments by the rates at which they are expected to run off or be drawn down over the next 30 days under conditions of stress, individual or systemic. The higher the rate applied, the greater the expected outflows relative to the available outstanding balances. In calculating the expected cash outflows, it should be noted that:

- Deposits and funding operations are distinct, both according to their maturity (less than or equal to 30 days or more) and depending on the type of transaction (not guaranteed and guaranteed), the counterpart (retail customers—including small retail businesses—or other customers, defined as wholesale), the type of relationship (operational or not) and the consequent level of stability in the supposed case of individual or systemic crises;

- Undrawn commitments that are contractually irrevocable or conditionally revocable are treated differently according to the counterparty (retail, wholesale excluding financial companies, and financial companies) and the intended purpose (credit or liquidity facilities);
- Possible downgrade of the bank by up to three notches can give rise to triggers embedded in financial transactions that require the automatic provision of collateral, resulting in additional cash outflows to be considered;
- Further commitments and off-balance sheet exposures specifically identified (structured finance instruments used by the bank, variations in the value of collateral in support of derivatives transactions and net payables derivatives) can result, in the case of individual or systemic crisis, in cash outflows that must be taken into account;
- From the combination of the above variables, for each type of funding operation, commitment or exposure, international regulation sets higher or lower weights. As already noted, the higher the weighting factors, the greater the expected cash outflows. The discretion of national supervisors is limited to obligations on facilities, market valuation changes on derivatives transactions and on other contingent liabilities like guarantees, letters of credit, revocable credit and liquidity (Table 4).

Total expected cash inflows are calculated by multiplying the outstanding amounts of on- and off-balance sheet receivables by the rates at which they are expected to flow in under the stress scenario up to an aggregate cap of 75 % of total expected cash outflows. The higher the rate applied, the greater the inflows than the current amount of on- and off-balance sheet items. In calculating the expected cash inflows, it should be noted that:

- The bank must consider only the contractual inflows from performing activities for which there is no reason to expect a breach within the time span of 30 days;
- In the case of reverse repos and securities borrowing maturing within 30 days, cash inflows are calculated differently, depending on whether the underlying security is a 'Level 1' asset, a 'Level 2' asset or another kind of asset not belonging to 'Level 1' or 'Level 2'[49];
- Irrevocable credit and liquidity facilities granted to the bank by other institutions are assumed to be unusable within 30 days and so they do not give rise to cash inflows. This is to prevent the risk of contagion and take into account that in situations of systemic stress the granting institution might not be able to keep its commitments;
- With the same logic, it is assumed that operational deposits held at other financial institutions (including those held at centralised institutions of a

---

[49] The goal is to prevent banks from exploiting double counting: if an asset is included in the stock of high-quality liquid assets, it cannot be computed as a possible source of cash inflows. For this reason, if the collateral is represented by 'Level 1' high quality liquid assets, the weighting factor is zero; if it is a 'Level 2' asset, the weighting factor is 15 %, and if it is an asset of another type, the factor is 100 %.

Table 4 Total net cash outflows calculation in LCR requirement

Cash outflows	Factor (%)	Cash inflows	Factor (%)
Retail deposits		*Reverse repos and securities borrowing maturing within 30 days, with the following as collateral*	
Stable deposits from natural persons, in transactional accounts or with other relationships that make withdrawal highly unlikely and covered by deposit insurance	5	Level 1 assets	0
		Level 2 assets	15
		All other assets	100
Less stable retail deposits from natural persons, not in transactional accounts or without other relationships or not covered by deposit insurance	10		
Term deposit with residual maturity greater than 30 days with a significant withdrawal penalty or no legal right to withdraw	0	*Credit or liquidity facilities*	0
		Operational deposits held at other financial institutions	0
Unsecured wholesale funding		*Deposits held at centralised institution of a network of co-operative banks*	0
Stable small business customers	5		
Less stable small business customers	10		
Legal entities with operational relationships (clearing, custody and cash management)	25	*Other inflows by counterparty*	
		Amounts receivable from retail counterparties	50
Portion of non-financial corporates, sovereigns, central banks and public sector entities deposits with operational relationships covered by deposit insurance	5	Amounts receivable from non-financial wholesale counterparties, from transactions other than those listed in the inflow categories above	50
Cooperative banks in an institutional network	25	Amounts receivable from financial institutions, from transactions other than those listed in the inflow categories above.	100
Non-financial corporates, sovereigns, central banks and public sector entities	75		
Other legal entity customers	100		
Secured funding maturing or callable within 30 days		*Net derivative receivables*	100
Secured funding transactions backed by Level 1 assets, with any counterparty	0		

(continued)

Table 4 (continued)

Cash outflows	Factor (%)	Cash inflows	Factor (%)
Secured funding transactions backed by Level 2 assets, with any counterparty	15	*Other contractual cash inflows*	National discretion
Secured funding transactions backed by assets that are not eligible for the stock of highly liquid assets, with domestic sovereigns, domestic central banks, or domestic public sector entities as a counterparty	25	Total inflows	
All other secured funding transactions	100		
Undrawn commitments contractually irrevocable or conditionally revocable to			
Retail and small business clients (credit and liquidity facilities)	5		
Non-financial corporates, sovereigns, central banks and public sector entities (credit facilities)	10		
Non-financial corporates, sovereigns, central banks and public sector entities (liquidity facilities)	100		
Financial (credit and liquidity facilities)	100		
Other contingent liabilities (guarantees, letters of credit, revocable credit and liquidity facilities)	National discretion		
Market valuation changes on derivatives transactions	National discretion		
Additional outflows related to derivative collateral calls related to a downgrade of up to 3 notches	100		
Additional outflows on collateral (other than Level 1 liquid assets) securing derivative transactions	20		
Outflows related to maturing ABCP, SIVs, SPVs, Conduits, etc.	100		
Net derivatives payable within 30 days	100		
Any other contractual cash outflows within 30 days	100		
Total cash outflows		Total net cash outflows = Total cash outflows − min {total cash inflows, 75 % of cash outflows}	

Source Based on Basel Committee on Banking Supervision (2010)

network of cooperative banks) cannot be used and therefore do not give rise to cash inflows during the following 30 days;

- For all other types of loans and amounts receivable within 30 days, the expected cash flows depend on the type of counterparty (retail customers, including small business customers, wholesale non-financial customers, financial customers). In the case of retail customers and wholesale non-financial customers, it is assumed that banks continue to extend loans—so as not to create financial management problems for customers—at a rate of 50 %, thus giving rise to a net inflow of 50 % of the contractual amount not renewed. In the case of financial customers, it is assumed that there is no renewal and that the related inflow is then equal to 100 %;
- In order to prevent excessive reliance on expected cash inflows to satisfy the LCR requirement and to ensure that banks hold a minimum level of liquid assets, the amount of inflows that can offset outflows is capped at 75 % of total expected cash outflows. Implicitly, this requires that a bank must hold a minimum stock of liquid assets equal to 25 % of the expected outflows;[50]
- For each category of outstanding balances of assets and off-balance sheet items, harmonized roll-off factors are set across countries with the aim of estimating the related inflows in the specified stress scenario, limiting national supervisors' discretion in the individual jurisdictions to the sole case of the other contractual cash inflows that are different from the previous (Table 4).

Banks, at least in the intentions of the BCBS, are expected to meet the LCR requirement continuously and on a consolidated basis.[51] The LCR will be calculated in one currency—the main currency of reference for the bank—and directed to the supervisor at least monthly. This metric, after an observation period, will be introduced as prescriptive starting from January 2015.

In the transitional period, it will be essential to monitor the interaction effects between the liquidity regulation based on the LCR requirement and differing central bank operational and collateral frameworks, particularly in terms of the securities that are eligible as lending facilities and the conditions for accessing the refinancing facilities. A recent empirical analysis showed the interaction between the new regulatory scheme based on the LCR metric with non-uniform operational and collateral frameworks among the various central banks, in terms of eligible securities and conditions for accessing the refinancing facilities. This interaction triggers potential regulatory arbitrage and can reduce the effectiveness of the new

---

[50] The total net cash outflows during the 30 calendar days are then calculated as follows:

$$Total\ net\ cash\ outflows\ =\ outflows\ -\ min\ \{inflows;\ 75\ \%\ of\ outflows\}.$$

This means that inflows are subject to an upper limit of 75 % of gross outflows, imposing in this way a requirement for banks to hold a minimum stock of high quality liquid assets at least equal to 25 % of gross outflows.

[51] During the implementation of the guidelines agreed by the Basel Committee, there may be differences between individual jurisdictions.

regulatory scheme. Central banks should therefore support the efforts of regulators to reduce the dependence of individual banks by refinancing with central bank institutions in managing their liquidity, through a redefinition and harmonization of eligible securities and access conditions that are currently very dissimilar across countries.[52]

4.2.2 The Net Stable Funding Ratio

The net stable funding ratio (NSFR) requires a bank to maintain, on a one-year horizon, a minimum amount of stable sources depending on the degree of asset liquidity, as well as the potential contingent liquidity needs arising from off-balance sheet commitments.

The objective of the NSFR is to ensure stable funding on an ongoing basis, over 1 year, in an extended firm-specific stress scenario where a bank can encounter: a disclosed significant decline in profitability or solvency arising from credit risks, market risks, operational risks or other risk exposures; a potential downgrade by recognized credit rating organisations; an event that puts at risk the reputation or the credit quality of the bank.

The NSFR operates as a minimum enforcement mechanism to complement the LCR, promoting structural changes in the liquidity risk profiles of banks by more stable, longer term funding of assets and business activities. In particular, the net stable funding ratio is structured to ensure that a bank holds an amount of stable liabilities that at least equals its medium-long term assets, taking into account their liquidity profiles:

$$\text{NSFR} = \frac{\text{available amount of stable funding}}{\text{required amount of stable funding}} > 1$$

The available amount of stable funding includes:

- Equity;
- Hybrid and debt instruments with effective maturities of 1 year or greater;
- A portion of non-maturity deposits, of term deposits and of wholesale funding with maturities of less than 1 year that would be expected to remain in the bank during an idiosyncratic stress event.

For the purposes of this standard, extended borrowing from central bank lending facilities outside regular open market operations is not considered in this ratio. This is to avoid creating a dependency on the central bank as a source of liquidity and to ensure that, in the case of an individual or systemic crisis, it performs a function of lender of last resort and not a function of first instance lender.

---

[52] Bindseil and Lamoot (2011).

The remaining contractual maturity of each operation is adjusted for any embedded options that could reduce maturity: it is assumed that all call options are redeemed at the earliest possible date.

Available stable funding is obtained by multiplying the bank's equity and liabilities balances by a factor representing the proportion of the balance that is expected to be available to the bank in 1 year to fund longer term assets: the higher this factor, the greater the stability of funding and the ability to support long term activity.

For each category, harmonized roll-off factors are set across countries in order to limit the discretion of the various supervisors in individual jurisdictions. In relation to these factors, one can observe that:

- For equity, hybrid instruments and liabilities with a maturity exceeding 1 year, full availability of the amounts is assumed;
- Deposits and funding sources on demand or at maturity equal to or less than 1 year are divided into stable and unstable, assuming the same criteria used for the calculation of the LCR requirement and distinguishing retail customers (including small business customers), wholesale non-financial customers and financial customers, which correspond to different weighting factors;
- All other liabilities are considered to be unavailable (Table 5).

The required amount of stable funding for assets and off-balance sheet exposures is the sum of the value of the assets held by the bank and the value of off-balance sheet activity, both multiplied by factors able to approximate the amount that could not be converted into cash on an extended basis during a liquidity event lasting 1 year: thus, higher liquid assets have lower factors (which could even be equal to zero) and require less stable funding available to the bank.

Even in this case, factors are almost totally preset to avoid differences among jurisdictions. However, if for liquid assets or for assets with a maturity within a year we would in theory expect a weighting factor of 0 % and for those with maturities of more than 1 year a weighting factor of 100 %, the new regulatory framework introduces a reality that is considerably more complex. It is interesting to note that some assets with medium-long term maturity will enter into the calculation of the stable assets with much reduced weights, while other assets with a maturity lower than 1 year may be considered stable:

- Government bonds with a maturity of more than 1 year and with a 0 % risk weight under the Basel II standardised approach are considered stable for 5 % of their amount, as it is assumed that it is always possible, even in the most difficult phase of the secondary market, to proceed to their conversion into cash, at least through central bank facilities;
- In the case of bonds issued by non-financial companies and covered bonds with a maturity equal to or exceeding 1 year and rated at least AA-, as well as for government bonds and similar with maturity equal to or higher than a year and with a 20 % risk weight under the Basel II standardised approach, the factor is 20 %;

Table 5 Required and available amount of stable funding in NSFR

Available stable funding (sources)		Required stable funding (uses)	
Item	Availability factor (%)	Item	Required factor (%)
Tier 1 and Tier 2 capital instruments	100	Cash	0
Other preferred shares with an effective maturity of 1 year or greater	100	Short term unsecured actively-traded instruments (<1 yr)	0
		Securities with exactly offsetting reverse repo	0
Other liabilities with an effective maturity of 1 year or greater	100	Securities with remaining maturity <1 yr	0
		Non-renewable loans to financials with remaining maturity <1 yr	0
Stable deposits of retail and small business customers (non-maturity or residual maturity < 1 yr)	90	Debt securities issued or guaranteed by sovereigns, central banks, BIS, IMF, EC, non-central government, multilateral development banks with a 0 % risk weight under the Basel II standardised approach	5
Less stable deposits of retail and small business customers (non-maturity or residual maturity < 1 yr)	80	Unencumbered non-financial senior unsecured corporate bonds and covered bonds rated at least AA-, and debt that is issued by sovereigns, central banks, and public sector entities with a risk-weighting of 20 %; maturity ≥ 1 yr	20
Wholesale funding provided by non-financial corporate customers, sovereigns, central banks, multilateral development banks and public sector entities (non-maturity or residual maturity < 1 yr)	50	Unencumbered listed equity securities included in a large cap market index	50
		Non-financial senior unsecured corporate bonds (or covered bonds) rated from A+ to A-, maturity ≥ 1 yr	50
		Gold	50
		Loans to non-financial corporate clients, sovereigns, central banks, and PSEs with a maturity <1 yr	50

(continued)

Table 5 (continued)

Available stable funding (sources)		Required stable funding (uses)	
Item	Availability factor (%)	Item	Required factor (%)
All other liabilities and equity not included above	0	Unencumbered residential mortgages of any maturity and other unencumbered loans, excluding loans to financial institutions, with a remaining maturity of 1 year or greater that would qualify for the 35 % or lower risk weight under the Basel II standardised approach for credit risk	65
		Other loans to retail and small business customers having a maturity <1 yr	85
		All other assets	100
		Off-balance sheet exposures: undrawn amounts of committed credit and liquidity facilities that are contractually irrevocable or conditionally revocable	5
		Off-balance sheet exposures: other undrawn commitments and other contingent funding obligations	National discretion

Source Based on Basel Committee on Banking Supervision (2010)

- For bonds issued by non-financial companies and covered bonds with a maturity equal to or exceeding 1 year and rated between A+ and A−, there is a factor of 50 %;
- For listed stocks issued by non-financial companies and included in the main large-cap indices, the weighting factor is 50 %;
- Loans to non-financial customers with a maturity lower than 1 year (excluding individuals and small retail businesses) have a weighting factor of 50 %;
- In the case of loans with a maturity of less than 1 year to retail customers— including small business customers—an 85 % factor is applied;
- For unencumbered residential mortgages of any maturity, excluding loans to financial institutions, with a remaining maturity of 1 year or greater that would qualify for the 35 % or lower risk weight under the Basel II standardised approach for credit risk, the weighting factor is 65 %;
- In the case of undrawn amounts of committed credit and liquidity facilities that are contractually irrevocable or conditionally revocable, the weighting factor is 5 % (Table 5).

An analysis of the previous weighting factors shows that even assets with a residual maturity of less than 1 year can be considered stable, while some assets with long term maturities enter into the calculation of stable activities with very low weights. For instance, exposures to small and medium-sized enterprises with a maturity of less than 1 year are considered to be stable for 85 % of their balances, a value that falls to 50 % in the case of large enterprises.[53] On the contrary, government bonds and similar securities with a maturity of more than 1 year are considered stable for 5 % of their amount, as it is assumed that it is always possible to proceed to their conversion into cash, at least through central bank facilities.[54]

Banks, at least in the intentions of the Basel Committee, have to meet the requirement of an NSFR that is higher than one continuously and on a consolidated basis.[55] The NSFR will be calculated in a single currency—the main currency of reference for the bank—and will be reported at least quarterly. After an observation period, this metric will become mandatory by January 2018.

---

[53] Small business customers, consistent with the definition already taken by the regulatory portfolios in Basel II rules, include non-financial small business customers that are managed as retail exposures with an aggregated funding raised from one small business customer that is, even on a consolidated basis, less than one million euros.

[54] This prediction requires that Government bonds or similar securities have a 0 % risk weight for credit risk under the Basel II standardised approach.

[55] As with the LCR requirement, even in this case, in the implementation phase of the reform, there may be differences in individual jurisdictions.

4.3 *Monitoring Tools to Assess Liquidity Risk*

Together with the sound principles and the two above minimum standards, BCBS has identified a number of parameters to be used by supervisors as an additional tool for continuous and consistent monitoring of banks' liquidity conditions. These metrics include:

- Contractual maturity mismatch that identifies the gaps between contractual inflows and outflows of liquidity over set time bands;
- Concentration of funding in order to detect those sources of wholesale funding (counterparties, instruments or currencies) that can trigger liquidity problems in the case of withdrawal;
- Outstanding balances of available unencumbered assets that can be used as collateral for secured borrowing or are eligible for central banks' standing facilities, supporting maturity mismatches and liquidity needs;
- Liquidity coverage ratios by significant currencies (higher than 5 % of the bank's total liabilities) that complement the LCR minimum standard calculated in one single currency, unveiling mismatches between high-quality liquid assets and total net cash flows in each relevant currency;
- Market-related metrics that use market information to capture early warning signals of potential liquidity difficulties.

By using these tools, supervisory authorities should be able to capture early signals of a potential liquidity problem by observing a negative trend in one of these metrics.[56]

5 Economic and Managerial Effects of the New Regulation

The new rules on liquidity risk will have a significant impact on the management of the bank. The main effects—some of which are already occurring—will concern:

- Profitability;
- Composition of assets and the business mix;
- Composition of liabilities;
- Replacement between banking and financial products;
- Further loss of market share in favour of the so-called "shadow banks".

---

[56] Basel Committee on Banking Supervision (2010).

5.1 The Impact on Profitability

In recent decades, at a time of increasing internationalization of financial systems and increasing competitive pressures, each bank had to strike a delicate balance between a prudent and harmonious maturity structure of assets and liabilities and the pursuit of appropriate levels of profitability. The increasing competition and margin compression combined with sometimes excessive levels of risk appetite have prompted some banks to look for combinations of assets and liabilities that were more and more profitable, reducing to a minimum the holding of liquid assets and expanding dramatically the degree of maturity transformation. This has given rise to very different liquidity risk exposures across countries and within each country between different banks.

In the new regulatory framework, these differences will tend to be limited: in the trade-off between the need, first, to ensure sound and prudent behaviour by banks and, secondly, not to depress the profitability and competitive capacity, the new regulation has prioritized the need for stability at the expense of profitability.[57] In the new framework, the risk tolerance level of the individual bank against liquidity risk will play a less significant role than in the past in defining the degree of exposure to risk as a function of the economic objectives pursued by the bank. The new rules on liquidity risk management and, in particular, on the two minimum ratios tend in fact towards a much more uniform composition of assets, liabilities and, especially, the choice of asset-liability management, resulting in significant effects on banks' profitability through:

- Increased holding of liquid assets;
- Lower maturity transformation.

Compliance with the requirement in terms of the LCR in fact requires the maintenance of a greater volume of high quality liquid assets and, in this way, will have a limiting effect on profitability because it will assume the maintenance of excess reserves and, more generally, of an asset structure that favours liquidity objectives over profitability objectives.

Simultaneously and in addition, compliance with the requirement in terms of the NSFR will impose a greater rapprochement between the weighted average maturity of assets and of liabilities, thereby reducing the degree of maturity transformation. This will force banks to make greater use of medium-long term funding, which is more stable and more expensive, and/or to reduce their medium-long term assets.[58] Given a normal yield curve, characterised by an upward slope, reducing the maturity transformation activity will have a negative impact on bank profitability, partially damped by the perception of the increased stability of individual banks and the lower risk premiums demanded by the market on the more stable medium-long term funding.

---

[57] Blundell-Wignall and Atkinson (2010).

[58] Resti (2011).

It is an obvious fact that, within certain limits, more liquid banks can obtain lower risk premiums and benefit from the greater liquidity condition. However, beyond a certain limit, for any bank the benefits of increased liquidity are more than offset by the lower return on assets.

A recent study has analysed the relationship between bank profitability and liquidity and has concluded that the impact of liquidity on banks' profitability is strongly influenced by both the business model and the funding market characteristics.[59] In particular, this study comes to prove empirically that banks with more traditional business models—based mainly on the collection of deposits from non-financial customers and on providing loans with the originate-to-hold model—have lower optimal levels of liquidity than banks with non-traditional business models. In other words, the benefits of greater liquidity cease earlier for traditional banks than for banks with non-traditional business models. If this is true, the regulatory imperative to hold a greater volume of high-quality liquid assets would result in a reduction of profitability that varies depending on the business model adopted by individual banks and the type of activity primarily undertaken: in fact, the impact of the new rules is very different for traditional commercial banks, wholesale commercial banks, investment banks, banks specialized in leasing, factoring, consumer credit or in providing asset management and private banking services to customers.

The new regulation would therefore suffer from the limitation of taking a one-size-fits-all approach, with rules that treat banks with different business models the same way, and totally disregard the specific features of the market's reference collection of each bank, even if these characteristics play an important role in defining the optimal level of liquidity for each bank.

5.2 The Effects on Bank Assets Composition and the Business Mix

The fulfilment of the two minimum liquidity ratios will give rise to a strong change in banks' asset composition, with a greater weight of government bonds and a lower burden of loans and securities other than sovereign bonds. The new rules on liquidity risk management unearth the ancient problem of the relationship between government debt and bank liquidity, further accentuating the already significant commingling between banking risks and sovereign risks, and thus laying the basis for increased systemic risk.

Sovereign bonds have the double advantage of being considered, for any maturity, as highly liquid assets and not constituting stable assets.

In the calculation of the LCR metric, the government bonds of the bank's home country benefit from unlimited computability with a weighting factor of 100 %, regardless of maturity and rating. The implicit assumption is that the central bank

---

[59] Bordeleau and Graham (2010).

will always be available, even in times of imperfect functioning of the secondary market, to take them as a base for operations of last resort.

In the calculation of the NSFR metric, government bonds with a medium-long maturity fall within the less stable assets with a weighting factor of 5 % and require a modest stable funding to support them.[60] Those with maturity of less than 1 year do not constitute permanent assets and do not require stable funding at all.

By isolating this aspect, the new rules on minimum liquidity ratios will generate across countries banking systems that are more willing to buy securities issued by their own sovereign debtors than to support the economy through direct loans to households and businesses, something that prompts many observers to question whether the greater stability of the banks could determine a significant cost in terms of the capacity of the banking system to sustain the real economy, with a potential negative impact on economic growth over the medium-long term.[61]

In fact, the loans have a far more punitive treatment in the calculation of both the minimum liquidity ratios.

In the calculation of the LCR coefficient, it is assumed that customer loans due within 30 days will create inflows at 50 % of the amount, due to the alleged need to renew the remaining 50 % of the granted loans to ensure the operational continuity of the borrowers.

In the calculation of the NSFR coefficient, even loans with a residual maturity of less than 1 year are treated as stable assets at 85 % of the amount of the granted loans, in the case of retail customers and at 50 % of their amount, in the case of loans in the corporate segment. In both segments, loans with a maturity of 1 year or more are considered stable for 100 % of their amount.

It should also be noted that, because of the calculation of both the minimum ratios, there will be a further reduction of undrawn commitments available in the credit facilities and in the technical forms characterised by a certain flexibility in the use of funds by borrowers: in fact, a share of the undrawn funds are considered both as an outflow of cash within 30 days in the LCR calculation and as a stable asset in the NSFR computation.

The same rules will also encourage banks to increase their share of loans with shorter maturities, which are less demanding in the calculation of the NSFR and potentially advantageous for the computation of the LCR, as the inflows associated with customers' loans can partially reverse outflows in the calculation of net cash outflows under stress.

These two considerations make it possible to understand how the new set of rules will eventually transfer, at least partially, the risk of liquidity from banks to borrowers and, in particular, to non-financial companies, which, for a time, will

---

[60] This weighting factor operates for sovereign bonds or similar securities with a 0 % risk weight for credit risk under the Basel II standardised approach.

[61] Otker-Robe and Pazarbasioglu (2010), IIF (2010), EBF (2010).

face a reduction of the funds available for liquidity and credit facilities and a restraint on the average maturity of loans.[62]

Securities other than sovereign bonds will receive an intermediate treatment between bonds and loans.

In the calculation of the LCR, bonds issued by non-financial companies and covered bonds, both rated at least AA-, fall between the 'Level 2' of high-quality liquid assets, even with limitations of computability and a 15 % haircut. Stocks, by contrast, are not included in the high quality liquid assets, regardless of the size and depth of their market quotation, and neither are undertakings for collective investment, regardless of the underlying assets.[63]

In calculating the NSFR, bonds issued by non-financial companies and covered bonds both with a maturity longer than 1 year generate a demand for stable funds of 20 % or 50 % of their amount, depending on the rating assigned to them.[64] In reference to the calculation of the NSFR, quoted stocks issued by non-financial companies and belonging to the main large-cap indices are included among the stable assets at 50 % of their value.

In light of the new regulatory framework, the choice for treasury and liquidity management of banks will undergo profound structural changes. The introduction of new rules on liquidity is likely to produce a crowding-out effect on corporate bonds for the benefit of sovereign bonds. It is likely that, other conditions being equal, there may be an increase in spreads between corporate bonds and government bonds in favour of the latter. An increase in yield spreads is likely to be seen also within the category of government bonds, where those with 0 % credit risk weights under the standardised approach of Basel II will be rewarded at the expense of others.

Also remarkable is the crowding-out effect that the new rules will produce on bonds issued by banks and underwritten by other banks in the primary market, or by those repurchased in the secondary market. In the new regulatory framework, bank bonds are treated in even more severe terms than those reserved for non-financial corporate bonds, with a further potential pressure on spreads. The only exception is covered bank bonds, which are useful for the purposes of compliance with both indicators. In this respect, the favourite use of covered bonds by banks, however, may weaken the creditworthiness of unsecured debt, thus creating, other conditions being equal, a lower demand for unsecured bonds and a further rise in spreads.

Regulatory changes will have a profoundly different impact on each area of banking activity and will determine a significant change of business mix, especially when the effects of the new liquidity regulation are analysed together with those of the new capital requirements. By isolating the sole impact of the new

---

[62] Resti (2011).

[63] Basel Committee on Banking Supervision (2011).

[64] Bonds issued by banks and financial companies with a maturity longer than 1 year are considered stable assets for 100 % of their value.

liquidity framework, while in the past internal transfer prices used for funding the various banking activities reflected only the cost of funding and any embedded options associated with the individual operations, after the new regulatory framework takes place it will be necessary to incorporate within the internal transfer prices a "liquidity premium" that reflects the implicit cost in terms of liquidity each operation needs to hold.[65] The incorporation of costs associated with new regulatory constraints in the evaluation of the comparative convenience of each business area will inevitably result in a possible reorganisation of the bank's portfolio of activities.

5.3 The Effects on Bank Liabilities

Following the new rules on liquidity risk, banks' funding policies will also undergo significant changes. In the new regulatory framework, there will be strong pressure on medium to long term funding instruments, increased competition, especially in the retail sector, and markedly aggressive interest rate policies, which will make funding more expensive for banks and paradoxically less stable at the level of individual banks, as they will become more sensitive to the rate offered.[66]

In the calculation of the LCR coefficient, funding sources are distinguished primarily according to maturity lower or higher than 30 days. While funding sources with effective maturity of 30 days do not generate cash outflows in the case of individual or systemic stress, demand deposits and those with an effective maturity of 30 days or less generate cash outflows estimated in different ways according to the degree of stability, which depends on the nature of the counterpart (retail or other), the type of funding (guaranteed or not) and the relationship between the bank and the customer (transactional or not). The rates used to estimate runoff vary, as noted above, from a minimum of 5 % for the collection of stable retail customers to a maximum of 75 % for non-guaranteed funding by sovereigns, central banks, public sector entities and non-financial corporations (except for small business customers classified as retail). In the case of individuals, the lowest run-off rates apply to funding operations covered by deposit insurance schemes and based on transactional accounts (on which, for example, salaries or pensions are automatically credited) or with counterparties which have stable and consolidated relations with the bank, such as to make the withdrawal less likely due to the significant switching costs.[67] In the case of wholesale customers, the lowest run-off rates apply to funding operations covered by deposit insurance and to uncovered accounts relating to operational relationships between banks and

---

[65] Sironi (2011).

[66] Otker-Robe and Pazarbasioglu (2010).

[67] Ruozi and Ferrari (2005).

clients (on which banks offer clearing, custody or cash management services to customers).[68]

In order to calculate the NSFR coefficient, it is necessary to distinguish the funding sources according to their maturity more than 1 year or less than one. Funding with a constraint length equal to or greater than 1 year is considered totally stable funding available to support the bank's activities in the medium-long term, and a weighting factor of 100 % is applied. The funding sources that are on demand or with a maturity of less than 1 year are treated differently depending on the counterpart: in the case of retail customers, it is necessary to distinguish, by following the same logic as the LCR requirement, between stable funding, which applies a weighting factor of 90 %, and less stable funding, which is associated with a factor of 80 %; for wholesale customers, regulation assumes a lower stability in a crisis situation and the weighting factor is set at 50 %.

The rules described above will give rise to deep changes in the qualitative objectives of the funding policy of the banks and will force a search for greater stability of funding in accordance with the new regulatory framework.

For deposits with a monetary function, it will be crucial to establish lasting relationships with customers who are increasingly focused on the long term and based on a constant monitoring of achievements, not only in terms of customer retention but also in terms of customer migration.[69]

For funding instruments without monetary functions, the search for greater stability will undergo a significant change in the mix of technical forms used by banks, with a progressive reduction in the role of non-cash deposits at sight, a greater use of non-monetary medium-long term deposits and an increasing use of bond issuance, either in the traditional unsecured version or in the covered version.

5.4 The Substitution Effects Between Banking and Financial Products

The increasing use of bonds and other instruments that provide more stable funding for banks will have important repercussions on the placement of those financial products distributed in the retail market through bank branches, with consequences on both macroeconomic and microeconomic levels.

The need to meet new minimum liquidity ratios—and, in particular, in this respect the NSFR—will have an obvious impact on the distribution to customers of certain financial products and instruments: mutual funds, separated accounts and

---

[68] Basel Committee on Banking Supervision (2010).

[69] The concept of customer migration, introduced by McKinsey, refers to all those cases of customers who, while not disrupting the relationship with the bank, move the bulk of their purchases to competing banks. These customers, while being "retained", would create greater losses in certain sectors (including the banking sector) than those resulting from non-retained customers. Coyles and Gokey (2002).

other asset management products, pension funds will suffer a kind of cannibal-ization by deposits, banking bonds and other direct funding instruments that are more stable and better able to ensure compliance with the new rules on liquidity.

This effect will have consequences on the structure of the financial system and the composition of financial portfolios of investors.

At the macro level, especially in those markets where banks are the largest distributors of such products, there will inevitably be less space for the placement of these instruments, with a significant impact on the size of the stock and bond markets and a consequent weakening of financial markets, due to the reduction in the number of actors and investors.

At the micro level, again more markedly in those systems in which banks are the main distributors of such products, the result will be a significant impact on the composition of the portfolios of retail customers, with possible inefficient allo-cation of the financial wealth of households and a consequent weakening of the risk-return combinations of their investment portfolios, because of the excessive weight of banking liabilities products, insufficient diversification of risk and a disproportionately low weight of risky assets.

The substitution effect between banking and financial products will then have a major impact on the placement of insurance products with a financial content that, similarly to mutual funds, separated accounts and pension funds, will undergo an effect of "crowding out" by bank deposits and by other direct funding instruments with the necessary strategic rethinking of bancassurance models adopted so far. In this way, insurance companies will suffer from a resize of bank branches as a distribution channel, that in some countries plays a very important role in the placement of many insurance products.

5.5 The Further Loss of Market Share in Favour of the So-Called "Shadow Banks"

The new rules on liquidity risk—even more so when considered together with the new regulation on capital adequacy of banks—will lead to a further strengthening of the role of so-called "shadow banks" as an allocation circuit of financial resources parallel to the official one. The "shadow banking" system covers all the subjects and activities that give rise to credit intermediation that complement and compete with those of the regular and supervised banks.[70]

These shadow banks can offer activities that are functionally capable of responding to the needs of the typical banking products and in particular: the collection of funds through instruments with economic characteristics similar to deposits; maturity transformation through use of funds on demand or at short notice for the granting of medium-long term loans; the transformation of illiquid

---

[70] Pozsar et al. (2010).

and non-tradable instruments into liquid and negotiable instruments; credit risk transfer from one person to another; the direct or indirect use of financial leverage. Examples, while not exhaustive, of these subjects are: money market open-ended funds, investment funds which directly or indirectly grant loans or use financial leverage; an array of non-bank intermediaries that grant loans, provide credit guarantees or carry out a function of maturity transformation; special purpose vehicles which, through securitisation, realize a transformation of maturities and liquidity; insurance companies issuing or guaranteeing credit risk related products.[71]

The activities of the shadow banking system are functionally directed to credit intermediation between surplus and deficit subjects and are based on the collection of instruments with similar characteristics to deposits and/or lending through repurchase agreements, securities lending and securitisation.

At the end of 2010 the overall value of the shadow banking system was estimated at 60,000 billion dollars, with a weight of more than one fourth of the total assets of the global financial system. These cumulative data, however, conceal a significantly different picture of the shadow banking in various countries, with weights, in some areas, even exceeding the role of the official banking system.[72]

The shadow banking system has undeniably played a role in facilitating access to credit by non-financial companies, expanding funding opportunities, taking advantage of economies of specialization and of various types of cost economies, and encouraging, at least in the short term, economic growth. However, this was done without respect to international and domestic rules governing the conduct of banking business, creating an alternative circuit of finance that is at the same time complementary and in competition with the banking system.[73]

The shadow banking system has been complementary to the regular banking system, because the same banks have made extensive use, especially in some countries, of this system in order to exploit arbitrage opportunities and to circumvent the rules on overseeing the safety and stability of banks, in search of further opportunity for profit.

At the same time, shadow banking has been in competition with the regular banking system because in some cases, just relying on the absence of rules and on the lack of severe supervisory controls, the shadow banks have stolen market share and customers from traditional banks, through the provision of products and services that are able to satisfy the same needs as traditional banking products.

In the absence of effective regulation of the shadow banking system, that can, on the one hand, prevent such unfair competition with the banks, and, on the other hand, eliminate regulatory arbitrage opportunities associated with the use of these subjects also by the same banks, the new prudential regulations on liquidity—together with those on bank capital requirements—run the risk of a further shift of

---

[71] FSB (2011a).

[72] FSB (2011b).

[73] European Commission (2012).

market share from traditional banks to shadow banks, further fueling an alternative circuit to allocate financial resources that complement or compete with the official one, and thus creating an additional source of systemic risk.

6 Conclusions

The integration of capital markets has undoubtedly facilitated the spread to the entire world economy of financial problems that were originally limited to some countries. However, these problems have arisen and have proliferated mainly because of regulatory gaps, distorted incentives, a strong underestimation of risk and reckless—when not explicitly fraudulent—behaviour.

Since liquidity risk is difficult to measure and depends on so many factors, a defence based on capital requirement is ill-suited to prevent it.

In recent decades, and until the summer of 2007, markets were characterised by high levels of liquidity and the increasing use of innovative financial instruments. If, on the one hand, the transformation of the international banking system in recent years has increased the technical solutions available to banks to manage liquidity risk, on the other hand, it has led to a major underestimation of the actual exposure to this risk.

Proper liquidity management policy requires examining the liquidity risk as a function of the impact area, the time horizon of the analysis, the origin and economic scenario where the risk occurs. After analysing these four aspects, it is necessary to define models of risk measurement, by identifying indicators to monitor and setting the appropriate operating limits that allow advance detection of the early signals of any potential liquidity crisis. In both the short and medium-long terms, each bank will have to address methodological choices related to the modelling of cash flows related to on- and off-balance sheet items that are char-acterised by a contingent nature in their use or repayments by customers.

Different methodologies have to hypothesize a normal business scenario, characterised by a stable market situation, and stressed scenarios, characterised by liquidity pressures at the company or systemic level.

Even the related organisational aspects are complex and vary depending on the model adopted by individual banks and, especially, the banking groups they belong to.

Regardless of the methodology used and the organisational models adopted, the choices regarding the management of liquidity risk are influenced by the risk appetite of each bank. At a time of increasing internationalization of the banking systems and greater competitive pressures, each bank had to strike a delicate balance between a harmonious maturity structure of assets and liabilities and the pursuit of increasing levels of profitability. This has given rise to liquidity risk exposures that differ greatly between the various banking systems and, within each system, between different banks.

The same supervisory activities in many countries were not so effective: it was thought that the increased complexity of the financial system could be managed and controlled with self-regulation alone, trusting in the internal management, control and reporting systems of the banks. The crisis has highlighted the weaknesses of these supervision models and has made it necessary to integrate domestic and international regulations to take into account that the search for bank stability and the reduction of competitive inequalities also requires the definition of a common set of rules limiting the liquidity risk appetite of banks.

Despite the long period for adaptation to new requirements, banks have already begun a thorough analysis of their balance sheets and their liquidity condition in order to initiate the necessary adjustment process and putting into effect all available instruments. Some banks have already embarked on a path that aims to gain increased efficiency, streamline processes, strengthen the capacity to collect funds, better oversee the risks and operate effectively in a context that is certainly more difficult, more competitive and more regulated.

Overall, empirical investigations indicate that the new regulation will help make the financial system more robust, stable and resilient to idiosyncratic or systemic shocks, albeit at a price—in terms of economic growth and capacity of the banking system to serve the real economy—that is not easy to assess, especially if one considers the joint impact of new rules on liquidity and the strengthening of the capital requirements imposed by the new capital accord.

The adjustment will certainly not be easy and will require a new balance between the profitability and riskiness of the business model that can withstand in a context of the "New Normal" of the economy and the financial system, characterised by contained economic growth, high unemployment rates, a gradual deleveraging, and economic performance of enterprises, including banks, that will be less brilliant than before.

References

Adrian T, Shin HS (2008) Liquidity and leverage. Federal Reserve Bank of New York. Staff Report, n. 238, May, revised December 2010 http://www.newyorkfed.org/research/staff_reports/sr328.pdf. Accessed 15 June 2012

Amihud Y, Mendelson H, Pedersen LH (2005) Liquidity and asset prices. Found Trends Financ 1(4):269–364

Angelidis T, Benos A (2006) Liquidity adjusted value-at-risk based on the components of the bid-ask spread. Appl Financ Econ 16(11):835–851

Bangia A, Diebold FX, Schuermann T, Stroughair J (2001) Modeling liquidity risk, with implications for traditional market risk measurement and management. In: Figlewski S, Levich R (eds) Risk management: the state of the art. Kluwer Academic Publishers, Amsterdam

Banks E (2005) Liquidity risk. Managing asset and funding risk. Palgrave Macmillan, Houndmills

Banque de France (2008) Special issue on liquidity. Financ Stab Rev 11:1–163

Basel Committee on Banking Supervision (1992) A framework for measuring and managing bank liquidity. Bank for International Settlements, Basel, September. http://www.bis.org/publ/bcbs10b.pdf. Accessed 15 June 2012

BCBS-Basel Committee on Banking Supervision (2000) Sound practices for managing liquidity in banking organisations. Bank for International Settlements, Basel, February. http://www.bis.org/publ/bcbs69.pdf. Accessed 15 June 2012

BCBS-Basel Committee on Banking Supervision (2008) Liquidity risk. Management and supervisory challenges. Bank for International Settlements, Basel, February. http://www.bis.org/publ/bcbs136.pdf. Accessed 15 June 2012

BCBS-Basel Committee on Banking Supervision (2010) Basel III—international framework for liquidity risk measurement, standards and monitoring. Bank for International Settlements, Basel, December. http://www.bis.org/publ/bcbs188.pdf. Accessed 15 June 2012

BCBS-Basel Committee on Banking Supervision (2011) Basel III framework for liquidity—frequently asked questions. Bank for International Settlements, Basel, December. http://www.bis.org/publ/bcbs211.pdf. Accessed 15 June 2012

BCBS-Basel Committee on Banking Supervision: Basel II (2006) International convergence of capital measurement and capital standards: a revised framework—comprehensive version. Bank for International Settlements, Basel, June. http://www.bis.org/publ/bcbs128.pdf. Accessed 15 June 2012

Bervas A (2006) Market liquidity and its incorporation into risk management. Banque de France. Financ Stab Rev 8:63–79

Bindseil U, Lamoot J (2011) The Basel III framework for liquidity standards and monetary policy implementation. SFB 649 Discussion Paper 2011-041. http://sfb649.wiwi.hu-berlin.de/papers/pdf/SFB649DP2011-041.pdf. Accessed 15 June 2012

Bini Smaghi L (2010) Basel III and monetary policy, international banking conference "matching stability and performance: the impact of new regulations on financial intermediary management. Milan, 29 Sept

Blundell-Wignall A, Atkinson P (2010) Thinking beyond Basel III: necessary solutions for capital and liquidity. OECD J Financ Mark Trends 1:9–33

Bordeleau E, Graham C (2010) The impact of liquidity on bank profitability. Bank of Canada Working Paper 2010-38, December. http://www.bankofcanada.ca/wp-content/uploads/2010/12/wp10-38.pdf. Accessed 15 June 2012

Borio C (2000) Market liquidity and stress: selected issues and policy implications. BIS Quart Rev 11:38–51

Bruni F, Llewellyn D (eds) (2009) The failure of northern rock: a multi-dimensional case study. SUERF—The European Money and Finance Forum, Vienna

Brunnermeier MK, Pedersen LH (2009) Market liquidity and funding liquidity. Rev Financ Stud 22:2201–2238

Bundesbank Deutsche (2008) Liquidity risk management at credit institutions, Deutsche Bundesbank. Mon Rep 9:57–71

CEBS-Committee of European Banking Supervisors (2007) First part of CEBS's technical advice to the European Commission on liquidity risk management. http://www.eba.europa.eu/getdoc/35ae99ee-dcee-4106-bd9b-cbf0ef8ad051/CfA_8_LiquidityStockTakesurvey.aspx. Accessed 15 June 2012

CEBS-Committee of European Banking Supervisors (2008) Second part of CEBS's technical advice to the European Commission on liquidity risk management. http://www.eba.europa.eu/getdoc/bcadd664-d06b-42bb-b6d5-67c8ff48d11d/20081809CEBS_2008_147_(Advice-on-liquidity_2nd-par.aspx. Accessed 15 June 2012

CGFS-Committee on the Global Financial System (2010) Funding patterns and liquidity management of international active banks, Basel, May. http://www.bis.org/publ/cgfs39.pdf. Accessed 15 June 2012

Coyles S, Gokey TC (2002) Customer retention Is not enough. McKinsey Quart 2:81–89

Deutsche Bundesbank, BaFin (2008) Liquidity risk management practices at selected German Credit Institutions. http://www.bundesbank.de/download/bankenaufsicht/pdf/liquiditaetsrisikomanagement.en.pdf. Accessed 15 June 2012

EBF-European Banking Federation (2010) EBF comments on the Basel Committee's consultative document entitled "international framework for liquidity risk measurement, standards and monitoring. 16 April. http://www.bis.org/publ/bcbs165/ebfl.pdf. Accessed 15 June 2012

ECB-European Central Bank (2007) Liquidity risk management of cross-border banking groups in the EU. EU Bank Struct 10:19–38

European Commission (2012) Green paper, shadow banking, Brussels, 19 March. http://ec.europa.eu/internal_market/bank/docs/shadow/green-paper_en.pdf. Accessed 15 June 2012

FSB-Financial Stability Board (2011a) Shadow banking: scoping the issues. A background note of the financial stability board, 12 April. http://www.financialstabilityboard.org/publications/r_110412a.pdf. Accessed 15 June 2012

FSB-Financial Stability Board (2011b) Shadow banking: strengthening oversight and regulation. recommendations of the financial stability board, 27 October. http://www.financialstabilityboard.org/publications/r_111027a.pdf. Accessed 15 June 2012

Garleanu N, Pedersen LH (2007) Liquidity and risk management. Am Econ Rev 97(2):193–197

IIF-Institute of International Finance (2007) Principles of liquidity risk management. Washington, March

IIF-Institute of International Finance (2010) Comments by the Institute of International Finance on the Basel Committee for banking supervision's consultative documents strengthening the resilience of the banking sector and international framework for liquidity risk measurement, standards and monitoring, Washington, April

IMF-International Monetary Fund (2006) Financial soundness indicators, Washington. http://www.imf.org/external/pubs/ft/fsi/guide/2006/pdf/chp8.pdf. Accessed 15 June 2012

Jarrow RA, Protter PE (2005) Liquidity risk and risk measure computation. Rev Futures Mark 11(1):27–39

Matz L (2007) Scenario analysis and stress testing. In: Matz L, Neu P (eds) Liquidity risk management. Wiley, Singapore

Matz L, Neu P (eds) (2007) Liquidity risk management. Wiley, Singapore

Murphy D (2008) Understanding risk. The theory and practice of financial risk management. Chapman & Hall/CRC Financial Mathematics Series, London

Nikolaou K (2009) Liquidity (risk) Concepts: definitions and interactions. Working Paper Series, European Central Bank, n. 1008, February. http://www.ecb.int/pub/pdf/scpwps/ecbwp1008.pdf. Accessed 15 June 2012

Onado M (2009) Northern Rock: Just the tip of the iceberg. In: Bruni F, Llewellyn D (eds) The failure of northern rock: a multi-dimensional case study. SUERF—The European Money and Finance Forum, Vienna

Otker-Robe I, Pazarbasioglu C (2010) Impact of regulatory reform on large and complex financial institutions. IMF Staff Position Note, International Monetary Fund, Washington, November. https://www.imf.org/external/pubs/ft/spn/2010/spn1016.pdf. Accessed 15 June 2012

Persaud A (ed) (2003) Liquidity black holes. Understanding, quantifying and managing financial liquidity risk. Risk Books, London

Pozsar Z, Adrian T, Ashcraft A, Boesky H (2010) Shadow banking. Federal Reserve Bank of New York, Staff Report No. 458, July, revised February 2012. http://www.ny.frb.org/research/staff_reports/sr458.pdf. Accessed 15 June 2012

Resti A (2011) Liquidità e capitale delle banche: le nuove regole, i loro impatti gestionali. Bancaria 11:14–23

Resti A, Sironi A (2007) Risk management and shareholders' value in banking. From Risk Measurement Models to Capital Allocation Policies. Wiley Finance, Chichester

Ruozi R (ed) (2011) Economia della banca. Egea, Milan

Ruozi R, Ferrari P (2005) La raccolta bancaria diretta. Tendenze evolutive, politiche, strumenti e dinamiche gestionali. Bancaria Editrice, Rome

Sironi A (2011) L'industria bancaria europea fra crisi economica e ri-regolamentazione. Quali strategie per il futuro? Economia Manage 5:3–8

SSG-Senior Supervisors Group (2009) Risk management lessons from the global banking crisis of 2008, October. http://www.fsa.gov.uk/pubs/other/SSG_risk_management_lessons.pdf. Accessed 15 June 2012

Stange S, Kaserer C (2008) The impact of order size on stock liquidity: a representative study. CEFS working paper No. 9. http://ssrn.com/abstract=1292304. Accessed 15 June 2012

The Joint Forum (2006) The management of liquidity risk in financial groups, Bank for International Settlements, Basel. http://www.bis.org/publ/joint16.pdf. Accessed 15 June 2012

Vento GA, La Ganga P (2009) Bank liquidity risk management and supervision: which lessons from recent market turmoil? J Money Invest Bank 10:79–126

Printed by Printforce, the Netherlands